TROP terrains +
open space

TROP terrains + open space

Works 2007–2023

Foreword by Boonserm Premthada

Introduction by Pok Kobkongsanti

Contents

14	Foreword	by Boonserm Premthada
16	Introduction	by Pok Kobkongsanti

- 20 **Ribbon Dance Park**   Xi'an, China
- 34 **Residence Rabbits**   Bangkok, Thailand
- 48 **Ashton Chula-Silom**   Bangkok, Thailand
- 60 **An Villa**   Shaoxing, China
- 76 **Veranda Pattaya**   Chonburi, Thailand
- 88 **Groove @ Central World**   Bangkok, Thailand
- 100 **Botanica Khao Yai**   Nakhon Ratchasima, Thailand
- 116 **Jing'An Century**   Shanghai, China
- 128 **Pyne by Sansiri**   Bangkok, Thailand
- 140 **J Residence**   Samutprakan, Thailand
- 152 **Ad Lib**   Bangkok, Thailand
- 164 **Quattro by Sansiri**   Bangkok, Thailand
- 176 **Urban Green Valley**   Shanghai, China
- 192 **Ashton Residence 41**   Bangkok, Thailand
- 202 **Hilton Pattaya**   Chonburi, Thailand
- 214 **Chiang Rai Residence**   Chiang Rai, Thailand
- 230 **Ashton Asoke-Rama 9**   Bangkok, Thailand
- 238 **Nana Coffee Roasters Bangna**   Bangkok, Thailand

- 251 Firm Profile
- 252 Awards & Project List
- 253 TROPSTERS
- 254 Project Credits

Foreword

I've known Attaporn, or Pocco as I call him, since 2012. We started chatting via Facebook Messenger after I read a story he wrote on Facebook about his attempts as a landscape architect. We exchanged words of encouragement and that was how I started to know him more personally in addition to his work. I see him as a black sheep (in a good way), someone who won't confine himself in a box, and most importantly, his personality is reflected in his work very well.

I have always believed that architecture, landscape, and interior architecture are one and the same, and if we can unite them, the work will come out just right. Every time I see Pocco's works, I see more than landscape. I see the architecture that exists in them and often little bits of interior architecture. Curves, straight lines, streams, bushes, bridges, every element in his work has a meaning and purpose. They are an atmosphere. And when we see photos of his works, we can imagine how it will feel to be there.

He cleverly integrates culture into his work. In one project in China, he incorporated a Chinese roof into the landscape, gently blurring the boundary of landscape and architecture. The Chinese roof cascading from the top, layer by layer, all the way to the ground, still fascinates me. It challenges those who see it to interpret the meaning it carries.

Many of his luxury residential projects in China are designed to warmly welcome members of the public to use and relax in the projects' gardens. The green space is for everyone, not just the residents in those lavish buildings. You can say that these are commercial projects, and I will say they are commercial projects with hearts.

Pocco's works are sustainable, protecting the ecological system and every tree in the ground, but he never uses sustainability as an excuse for an unattractive or less beautiful design. When I look at his work, I see beauty as an important function along with sustainability. He is an exemplary landscape architect whom future generation architects should learn from.

I once asked him if he wanted to teach. He hurriedly shook his head. If you follow him on social media, you will see that he writes and expresses his thoughts and opinions in a straightforward, intelligent way. His views, regardless of yours, are impossible to ignore.

And so, I sum up his works in one phrase: "More than Architecture."

Boonserm Premthada

Pok Kobkongsanti and Boonserm Premthada in shared conversation

Introduction

I am pleased to introduce you to this collection of TROP's work. It showcases the beauty and artistry of our designs, the restorative powers of nature, and the opportunities and possibilities for creating immersive and engaging landscapes in diverse settings. Reflecting on these projects, I am proud of what TROP has achieved and the landscapes we have crafted to provide people with a better outdoor experience.

When I started TROP in 2007, I wanted to develop unique landscape designs that were visually memorable and grabbed people's attention. But trying to create a signature design failed each time. Instead, I drew inspiration from my idol Bruce Lee describing his fighting philosophy:

> *"Empty your mind, be formless. Shapeless, like water. If you put water into a cup, it becomes the cup. You put water into a bottle and it becomes the bottle. You put it in a teapot, it becomes the teapot. Now, water can flow or it can crash. Be water, my friend."*

Rather than concentrating on the final appearance, we focus on the design process, and approach a brief without any preconceived notions. We are flexible and open-minded in how we explore ideas—formless and shapeless, like water. We let the context, architecture, program, and problems shape the solution. The solution then shapes the design. It consequently often results in something we never expected: a landscape we couldn't have envisioned without working through the layers of problems and solutions.

While our designs are still memorable, they grow from our desire to create spaces that add value to a neighborhood and improve the environment and the experience of the people who use it. Growing up in Bangkok, we didn't have many outdoor places to spend time, so we hung out inside or in shopping malls. At TROP, we want city dwellers to be comfortable and enjoy being outdoors and to have places the community feels connected to.

We are not seeking to solve the world's problems, but we are seeking to solve local problems and make the world better, little by little. I like to use the comparison of an ant carrying a small leaf: One ant, one leaf. Many ants, many leaves. By improving one site at a time, we provide a safer, more beautiful area for people to enjoy. The vegetation improves air quality by intercepting pollution, and it creates microclimates that offer relief from rising temperatures. Birds, bees, insects, and animals have new biodiverse habitats, and green space absorbs water and reduces runoff. Over time, individual sites flourish into a green network across a city and the positive effects compound. The urban environment is enlivened with plants, people, animals and insects, and the open spaces allow more natural light and ventilation amid the density of high-rise buildings and traffic-laden roads.

In designing a landscape, we envision ourselves as the people who will be using it. We imagine how they will experience it—what they will see, smell, hear, and feel; how they will move through the landscape, interact with others, and what activities they might do. The sequencing of spaces is orchestrated from the moment a person steps foot on the path or grass to how pathways, open areas, planting, features, seating, and views are choreographed. We want to draw them into the landscape, encouraging them to meander and inviting people to relax, discover, and explore.

Creating authenticity, locality, and microclimates are the basis of every landscape we design. We select plant species that belong to that particular environment—often ones that people see every day, but with attention to the setting and details, they become noticeable, and people appreciate the beauty in what was the ordinary. We draw inspiration from the geographical and urban context and cultural heritage of the site to create a landscape that belongs to its location. And we create pleasant microclimates that offer respite from heat, noise, and pollution. Textures and layers of vegetation lower the temperature, buffer the hustle and bustle of the city, and absorb pollution to provide cool, shady, and peaceful places for people to be outdoors. Then we add an intangible layer to further enrich the experience. Whether it is playing with nostalgia, tradition, or the senses, this evocative quality means every project is memorable and distinct.

What is the same, is our landscapes are always connected to architecture, and they live seamlessly together. The landscapes are the medium that grounds the architecture to the earth. We describe them as the 'roots' of a building, as if the building was a tree. And while the architecture will remain static and very gradually change, the landscape is a dynamic living background that continuously changes its forms and colors and animates the world around it.

Humans need to connect with nature—it's in our DNA. The landscapes we design are powerful, restorative places where visitors can have this connection and feel tranquil and refreshed. We hope this book offers you the same. That as you leaf through the pages, you will feel calm and relaxed. That the beautiful pictures will transport your imagination to a lush green space, and it will stir your love for nature and desire to connect with the earth.

Pok Kobkongsanti

terrains + open space

Ribbon Dance Park

Located in the new district of Qujiang, Xi'an, the Grand Milestone Art Centre was set to be the sales gallery and clubhouse for future development within the same plot. Comprising both public and private connotations, the client and design team sought to successfully promote pedestrian accessibility for both the visitors and local communities. The project boasts a sophisticated and intricate landscape wherein each garden and courtyard takes its place as a living background for the exhibited artwork. But for these wonders to be fully appreciated, visitors needed easy access to the site. We proposed the "Ribbon Dance Park," where a meandering ribbon-like boardwalk reconnects the existing footbridge and pavement with the new development, reinvigorating and adding value to the neighborhood.

The long, green corridor acts as the development's front yard. Here, the landscape team envisioned a transitional public park that slowly draws visitors into a fully immersive landscape experience. This boardwalk, extending above the new entry driveway and directing people to the nearby Xi'an botanical gardens, lightly touches the steeply sloping ground while meandering to create rooms and viewpoints of various sizes. The result is an ethereal boardwalk that emerges from the various green shades of the surrounding landscape. Finally, the park would not be complete without the uncomplicated yet ingenious selection of native grasses and cedar trees. The plants, rustling and softly bleeding into the pathway through the gaps between each balustrade, create a dynamic landscape that changes its forms and colors all year round.

RIBBON DANCE PARK

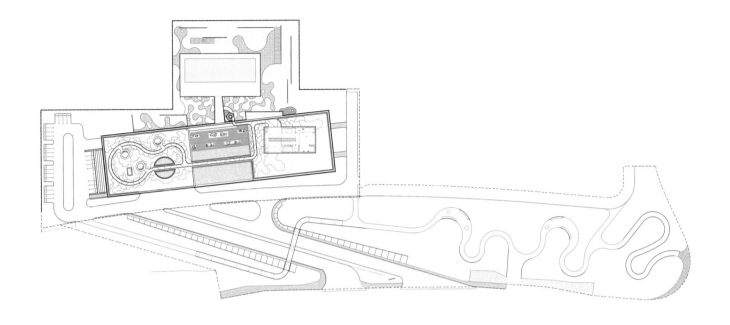

The Gallery Arrival Court is where the gallery welcomes all the visitors traveling by car. To create a powerful sense of arrival, the landscape team reinvented this drop-off point, turning it into an extraordinary "Court of Light." Instead of leaving the roundabout empty, tens of thousands of small, shiny aluminum plates, in collaboration with Two Tree Studio, float together in the form of a conceptual cuboid room that wraps around four exposed columns. A direct visitor's path from the sheltered parking area was added through the center of the subtracted spheric space within this room, creating a vista into the inner "Water Courtyard." Within the spheric extent lies a reflecting pool and a "Lonely Dancer" tree. In the daytime, the open roof above allows natural light to fill the space, creating an unending reflection involving the aluminum plates and water that shines onto the tree. At night, the lighting illuminates the spheric volume from below, producing an otherworldly stage that marks the great beginning of the visitors' journey into the gallery.

Leaving the Court of Light, visitors find themselves immersed in the sound of the waterfalls. This fully enclosed Water Courtyard displays a symmetrical arrangement of three landscape features: a straight path through the middle of a reflective pool, several groups of trees in various locations, and a series of long, multilevelled waterfalls on one side. The indoor gallery initially lacked full integration with the landscape as it was clearly separated from the Water Courtyard. To create an infinite continuity between indoors and outdoors, the landscape team proposed a modification to the gallery spaces by replacing some exhibition area with courtyards, permitting more natural light into the gallery. The single waterfall was transformed into a three-tiered cascading pool. Eighteen Sapium trees in total were planted throughout all six court gardens, creating a painting-like backdrop for various indoor exhibitions while complementing and softening the cascading waterfall structure seen from within the Water Courtyard. The result is the seamless connection between the architecture, interior spaces, and landscape that are all specially made for one another.

In the center of the rear garden lies another exhibit building, connected to the main gallery with an indoor walkway with floor-to-ceiling glass windows entirely opening up to the surrounding landscape. The garden ground is perceived as one giant canvas for an abstract painting: "The Magical Forest."

Inspired by interconnected blobs of paint, the soft, undulating mounds bleed into the entire space and display a tranquil tone. To maximize water retention in the dry climate of Xi'an, the landscape team filled the paths in between these mounds with gravel, creating an entirely porous garden. Deciduous trees with light foliage and sculptural forms are dispersed randomly within the area, creating a sparse forest but with almost consistent spacing. The forest animates the courtyards and adjacent interior spaces by filtering the sunlight with its ever-changing canopies through the seasons, and it stands firm as a multidimensional artwork itself.

The landscape team saw the flat roof of the gallery tower as the perfect platform for an artistic garden inspired by the dappling of colors in Monet's Impressionist paintings.

The meticulous planting design plays an essential role in the appearance of this garden. To display intricate contrasts of textures and colors all year-round, a great variety of winter-tolerant ornamental grasses are carefully interspersed throughout the roof extent, with evergreen grasses, perennial shrubs, and trees in selected places as the accents. The simplistic garden path forms a complete loop with smooth, undulating curves resembling the design language of the Ribbon Dance Boardwalk. At different points on the path, three circular seating spaces squeeze themselves into the grassy landscape, creating an outdoor room for the visitors to fully immerse in the field of various colors and textures around them. A striking white spiral staircase links both gardens.

Today, the Ribbon Dance Park is widely used by the local communities, with people strolling along the meandering paths or using the landscape for jogging, as a playground, or as an outdoor living room, generating a meaningful project for the district.

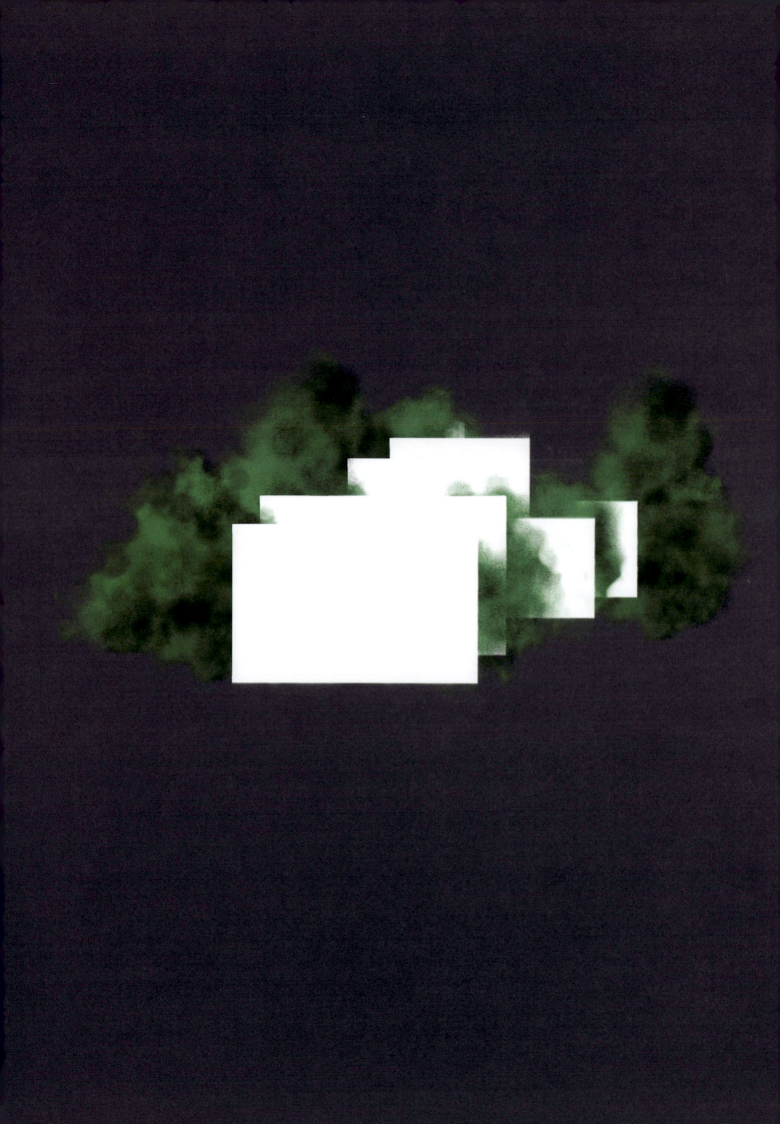

Residence Rabbits

Nestled in a quiet residential neighborhood of Bangkok, this house was designed for a landscape architect, his wife, and their young son, with a request for "a house with a series of courtyards." In addition, the design needed to accommodate the extreme climate, with the garden echoing the architecture language while also connecting to the home and creating pleasant microclimates. The landscape design offers a sensitive solution for an urban home, and fulfils the brief that the garden should be able to grow along with the family and their needs. Requests from the client were viewed as opportunities rather than problems, and have been translated into subtle yet creative design solutions.

The two-storied house, designed by Boon Design, occupies the site while leaving enough open space to accommodate a refreshing pool, large trees, as well as an inviting lawn. The relationship between the house and the landscape becomes crucial. By dividing the house into two closely interconnected volumes, it leaves room for the natural environment desired by the family. Each interior space is visually connected to different types of views outside, with views and amounts of sunlight all taken into account, and translated into differing sections of the surrounding landscape. With such relationship with the different "rooms" within the house, the landscape becomes a place for activities and experiences, responding to the inhabitants' actions and events that might occur from within, rather than trying to express any stylistic or geometric characters from without.

Cultivation and construction both demand different attitudes toward the terrain; more specifically, the first often refers to landscape design while the second to architecture. Yet the difference is not always prominent. Sometimes a project demonstrates a close relationship rather than distinction between the two. This residence design had as its goal this integral relationship, requiring a rethink again about the similarities between topographical cultivation and construction. We proposed a series of white solid walls along the east–west axis to help block the strong afternoon sunlight from the south. The rooms are integrated between these walls. With full-length glass windows, every room boasts two garden views toward the east and the west.

The garden was designed not only to echo the architecture language, but also to complement and accommodate the local climate. Overall, the courtyards create a variety of connections between the house and the garden. Together, the house and the garden create pleasant microclimates for the residents and their guests. To the inhabitants, this landscape is cultivated and constructed "for them," with activities smoothly flowing from one space onto the next. Indeed, it is not difficult to imagine differing spaces within the landscape grown and transformed, merging and emerging as lifestyles change over the years. Rather than a completed entity composed by the designer, the house's landscape is like a work in progress, waiting to be filled by the owners' future needs.

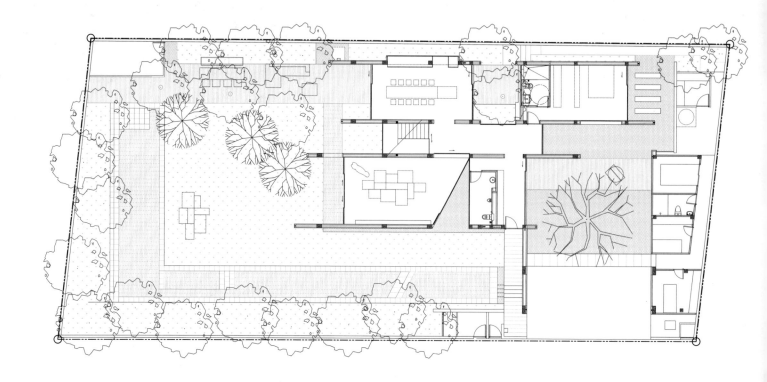

Working closely with its architecture, the landscape of this home springs from a design that sensitively engages the particularities of the site and will not satisfy itself with the invention and variation of abstractions. Everything is tangible, and provides a real platform for daily activities. At the same time, this platform—a stage for the prosaic activities of life—is at once familiar and inspiring, offering an escape into a selective dream. Considered as a unified whole, the house and its landscape can be seen as an ensemble that allows both the internal and external factors to come into play. Life, particularly a family life, always fluctuates and changes, and our design for this home reflects this. This is where a careful cultivation of landscape design and the construction of a residence truly become one.

Ashton Chula-Silom

This high-end residential building is located in the center of Bangkok's bustling urban district. Sitting on Rama 4 Road, one of the major arteries of the city, we needed to create for the residents a connection to nature while also promoting a better living environment. By maximizing green areas, drawing an inviting pedestrian passage, and providing a semipublic garden at the front, the landscape helps to blur the sharp line of this exclusiveness, thus contributing to the greening effort of the nearby streets and footpaths. The close collaboration with the architects, A49, and other consultants has also fostered a creative integration of landscape and architecture. The man-made "Green Mountain" wrapping the low-rise car park building is one of the essential features in response to the growing issues of urban heat island, glare effect, and increasing urban water runoffs.

Living in such a convenient and dynamic location comes with a high price, environmentally. The surrounding busy roads spout air and noise pollution. The surrounding density of the high-rise urban skyline means limited open spaces and ventilation. Well-aware of the challenges, the landscape team came up with a simple yet effective holistic greening approach. As a result, the landscape becomes an integral part of the design that could enliven this urban habitat again. The final design consists of three key landscape components: the Entry Garden, the Urban Mountain, and the Rooftop Multileveled Pool and Observation Deck.

ASHTON CHULA-SILOM

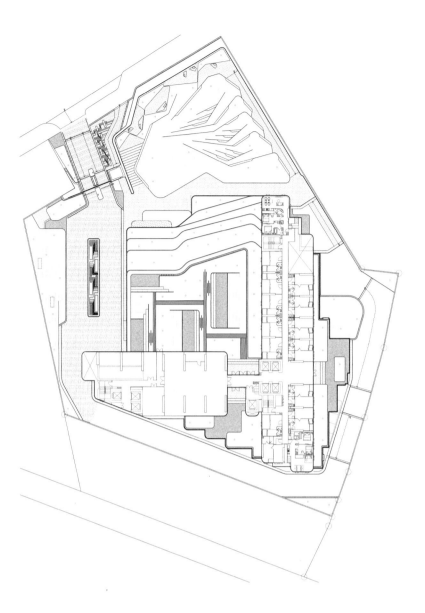

We established a smooth pedestrian access ramp at the entry level of the building to encourage the residents to use public transport and travel on foot. The pedestrian passage is lined with a feature wall on one side, and a shallow cascading water feature on the other to create a conceptual transition from the busier streets outside to the more relaxing garden inside. To try to work within the limited space, our team sought to limit paved driveway areas, maximize the soft landscape, and, in the process, create a sizable frontal sunken garden. Although merely consisting of a simple green area, a group of evergreen and deciduous trees, and a series of seat walls integrating into the undulating ground, this garden acts as the catalyst for the inclusive and seamless urban green connection in many ways. For instance, the low boundary wall allows for visual linkage, mitigating the impact of abrupt public and private segregation. The trees within the garden are planted close enough to form a future interconnected canopy with the existing street trees on the other side of the wall, providing continuous shade to the footpath. Lastly, the overall significant undulating soft landscape helps to counter heat absorption, reduce surface runoffs, and create a pleasant green environment for the tenants and commuters.

The low-rise front of the building houses an entry lobby, a coffee shop, and a five-story car park and forms the focal point of every approach. We saw an opportunity to cover the entire structure with plants, resembling a "Green Mountain" with various textures and foliage that breathes life into the bold, dark-colored, high-rise building behind. The plants in many forms and layers act as a soft shield protecting the building from absorbing too much heat, and the stepping terraces planted with trees also help to filter dust from the roads and help absorb pollution emanating from the car park. Before reaching the garden on its peak, these stepped terraces are intentionally created not for people but to provide a shelter to encourage visits from birds and bees.

The garden at the top of the Green Mountain screens the bare roof and prevents glare from disturbing the residents living above it. The prevalent use of softscape areas contrasts with the hardscape areas that exist in the form of sunken courtyards filled with gravel beds, which filter and convey water back into the surrounding softscape, successfully tackling the issue of stormwater discharge into the city's main pipes. These sunken gravel courtyards also break down the vast scale of the roof, creating rooms for various activities and encouraging more interaction among the residents.

ASHTON CHULA-SILOM

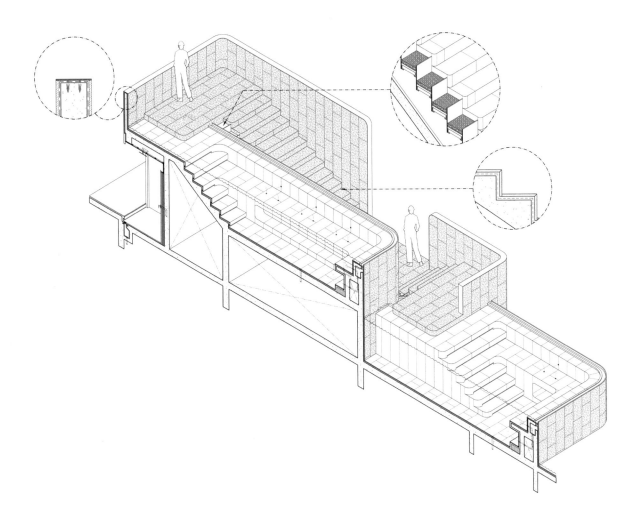

Covering most of the floor area on the 49th rooftop floor, the swimming pool takes full advantage of the unobstructed view of the city skyline by extending its arms out, allowing space for a proper lap pool, kids' pool, and Jacuzzis. The lap pool occupies the uninterrupted southern edge that opens up to the majestic and panoramic view of Bangkok's city skyline. Instead of placing one pool next to another on the same level, the landscape team thought beyond a flat plane and created a series of multitiered pools, with several Jacuzzis placed higher than the rest. The raised structures also free up extra room for other pool facilities such as outdoor showers and supporting mechanical systems. The use of light material colors in the pool underlines the simple rectangular forms and makes the pools seem larger than they are.

The rooftop gym and shared business center float above the pool level. Underneath the structure lies an observation deck consisting of several group seating areas. Framed by columns, these areas create semi-outdoor living rooms while also profiting from the extensive northeastern skyline. The plant selection here aims to soften the sharp building edges and reflect the amount of sunlight each area receives. Located further back under the building's overhang, more shade-tolerant shrubs with big leaves are widely used, while the spaces totally open to the sky are filled with flowering fine-leaved shrubs and trees, creating contrast in textures and a sensory garden. The simple rectangular designs and straight lines with rounded corners inspire the overall landscape composition. The forms, similar to the building's shape, are applied throughout the entire development, which helps to bind the architecture and landscape together and create a well-integrated urban living experience.

An Villa

At An Villa, situated in Shaoxing to the south of the Yangtze River, we wanted to honor the town and the associated memories it holds for its inhabitants over the years. The region is renowned for its significant rainfall, and the town is famous for its canal network, bridges, and picturesque alleys. Designed as an ode to the old Shaoxing, An Villa uses its internal landscape to manifest nostalgia and memories of rain in its architecture. Before we started considering the landscape concept design, our team sought first to understand the uniqueness of Shaoxing, including the urban and geographical context, as well as its historical background. We developed a deep affection for the village, with its idyllic scenes and we appreciated its simplicity and the relationship between the buildings and canals, as well as the link between its people and their landscape. We love the way the villagers integrate traditional design with their environment. Because of the high rainfall, people here tend to live under roofs and eaves. Not only do the roofs protect from the heavy rain, but they allow daily life and activities to continue, including drinking tea communally or enjoying the famous Shaoxing wine. People who grew up here always carry the memory of raindrops on the roof.

For the project, we decided to divide the landscape area into two main gardens. The first one sits in front of the villa. The second garden is a sunken space right in the middle of the villa's architecture. In order to create a garden with a sense of place, we carefully considered the relationship between the architecture and the site, the relationship between the people and the landscape, and the relationship between the architecture and hydrology. These three relationships guided the design of our garden at An Villa. For the first garden, the original context is a flat area right in front of the entry pavilion, which has a prominent roof feature. The left part of the area is a boundary wall. Being a residential project, we posed the question: what sort of garden did we want to create in this space?

Drawing inspiration from typical architectural roofs, we created a roof-like water feature at the arrival court to facilitate the departure and arrival experiences. We selected local roof tiles that had been in use in Shaoxing for centuries to capture the essence of the traditional building methodology, and hired local workers with their knowledge of how to use the material. Thus, local materials, local knowledge, and local techniques were all brought together to create something old and yet new at the same time. For this first entry garden, we selected a mainly ecological and natural planting, combined with exquisite spherical shrubs that impart a sense of sculpture. By creating a rain-like effect, this artistic installation has become the pride and pleasure of Shaoxing architecture and cultural heritage. We constructed an external wall of rough-textured, dark gray volcano stone wall that beautifully complements the stacking roof design. The overall view of the front garden represents a serene landscape.

For the second garden, the space was a box-like sunken area with tall retaining walls on three sides of the courtyard. We took into consideration the relationship between the roof and the runoff of water, and looked at how the rainwater in the old town was managed with a system of gutters and eaves. The final design allows for the excess water to pour down the channels of the roof tiles. The sequence of space is rhythmic and we used landscape walls, corridors, and plants to open and close the spatial relationships. The team employed a small amount of metal in our design judiciously to increase the artistic contrast of the textures. We used lush green planting that, when combined with the black tiles and metal, makes the space refreshing and evokes a calming atmosphere. Sitting in the courtyard, one is aware of the different layers of the landscape: the trees, the roof, and the contrasting tiles against the sky. On sunny days, the shadows of the trees cast a natural pattern on the man-made roof. The planting methods are mainly ecological natural planting combined with exquisite spherical shrubs with a sense of sculpture, and then the space is supported by tall trees with a sense of spatial volume and graceful shape to make it rich, exquisite, ecological, and colorful. When it rains, the water pours down the slope, while people can sit in the courtyard with a cup of tea, enjoying the sound of the showers. The network we designed drains water efficiently and prevents excess rainwater by allowing it a natural drainage channel. Our team called this second garden the "Roof and Rain Courtyard."

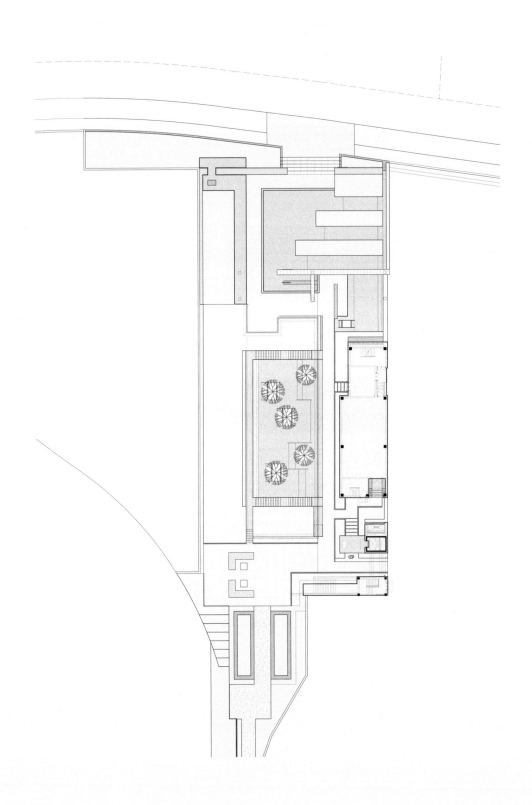

There's an old Chinese idiom that states "Fly over the eaves and run on the walls." It refers to a desire to become a great personage, powerful enough to climb away from the traditional house structure and over the roof. To this end, we provided a small pathway to one side for the residents to climb. As they ascend, the roof transforms from architecture to a landscape, offering different experiences at the various levels of the new sloping landscape. At the top level, we included a small pathway for both circulation and maintenance purposes. We designed these two gardens as a respectful nod to the architectural heritage of Shaoxing, and to evoke memories of the old town. The result is something that resembles a traditional roof of memory, yet also something that transforms into a new architectural motif not seen before.

Veranda Pattaya

With the increasing price of land, most of the beautiful beachfront plots have already been bought up by developers. Newly built beach resorts are therefore more likely to be placed on linear land with just one narrow side open to the beachfront. Our challenge in designing resorts now is to focus on how to create a memorable beach holiday experience while waterfront accesses are limited.

Located on Jomtien beach, away from chaotic central Pattaya, Veranda Pattaya is a new resort that represented an opportunity to work through this challenge. Like so many other new resorts, the site is linear shaped with one end connected to the ocean.

In addition, the site topography slopes, resulting in the beach access being much lower than the road entrance. To accommodate this drop, we built the lobby area one level down from the resort drop-off. The visitor can enter the hotel lobby by walking down the entrance staircase, or via the sloping landscape pathway. Surrounded by green hedges and ground cover, the reflecting pond with its stones is placed to deliberately echo the presence of the sea. The dining area is also located on the same level as the lobby. Berms covered with the native plant *Ipomoea pes-caprae*, or Beach Morning Glory, are used to create a green-surrounded outdoor dining area.

The two swimming pools are located toward the beachfront area, offering stunning views of the Gulf of Thailand. Employing a 'V' for Veranda motif, the two V-shaped Jacuzzis are integrated within the pool, along with three matching V-shaped sun beds. The two pools are separated by a shallow area, complete with added greenery, with ice-cream-stick-shaped stepping-stones that lead to the open seafront and add a playful element to the design. Returning to the main resort building, these unique stepping stones gently descend against a slatted surface with running water.

Three wooden slatted pavilions, complete with comfortable seating, emerge from the verdant hedge-like berm over the side walkway leading to the pool, and also providing access to the sun deck and to the beach. The other side of the far pool boasts four such wooden slatted pavilions, set at an angle.

We placed the sun deck facing directly to the sea, and used a mixture of grass and white gravel to decrease the impermeable area. Stone walls create a transition between the level of the swimming pool and the bar lounge below, and also act as protection against the risk of tsunamis. After studying the shape and motion of the waves, we decided to install a curved seawall that helps roll the waves without causing erosion to the site, thereby protecting the precious beachfront.

On the rooftop of the resort building overlooking the sea, we added a unique element to bring life to our concept of a sea journey. Building on this idea, we created a cantilevered deck with pier-like designs separated by water, with a lamp on each deck and sunken seat, acting as a lighthouse, and the foldable sail representing a ship's sail.

The overall design succeeds in accommodating the sloping site, thoughtful placement of resort elements, and injecting a playful element that ensures a memorable beach holiday.

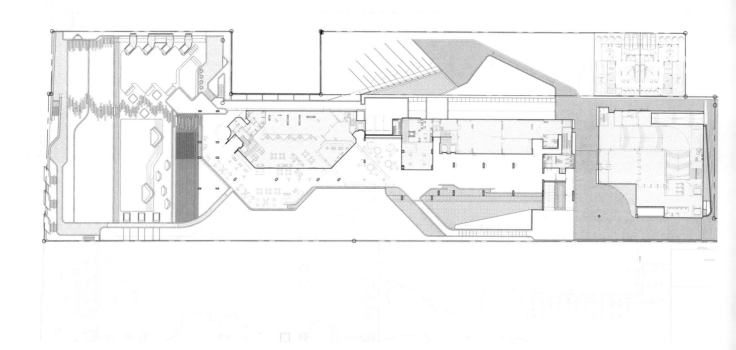

Groove @ Central World

Bangkok. A city with 15 million people and an estimated eight million vehicles. Add in to the mix a couple of million tourists and myriad street vendors who occupy the sides of the street and you have a pedestrian muddle. In some roads, the pedestrian circulation is completely blocked by either legal or illegal signage, forcing folk to walk on the street instead. So when our client for Groove @ Central World wanted us to design the landscape for their new retail project, they wanted it to be the "talk of the town." We went one further. Inspired by the city's lack of quality pedestrian walkways, we wanted to ensure that this project was the "walk of the town." Our goal was to design a good public pathway for the people of Bangkok.

Situated between two of Bangkok's busiest train stations, Groove @ Central World is a two-story retail space, on top of the client's existing parking building in a prime area of the city. Both train stations are connected to the city's largest shopping centers, with a huge number of pedestrians walking between the two each day. The existing car park structure was located next to public pathway. It was designed as a multilevel underground parking with a huge void between it and the footpath, allowing sunlight and air to penetrate. The lowest floor was about a 5-meter drop from the footpath, and needed guardrails to prevent people falling down into the void. The site had a number of mature royal palm trees, whose shade made it too dark to walk in the evening. A large portion of the footpath was used as parking for motorcycles. The overall effect was to create an area with a reputation for being cool and green.

GROOVE @ CENTRAL WORLD

Our original scope was to design the courtyard inside the new shopping mall. The client wanted the space to become the "talk of the town," in terms of commercial activities and overall 'wow' effect, in order to compete with their competitors (the other high-end malls in the area). The new mall was designed as a two-story building with a fluid façade. As it was built on an existing structure, the lowest floor was about 2 meters higher than the street level. The new structure is linked to the public footpath by small pathways that lead to the entrances, and so appears to be set apart. With these conditions in mind, our design team decided that our main task should focus on the area outside of the mall, and our goal would be to improve the walking environment.

The first thing to do was ensure that the existing royal palm trees were removed and replanted somewhere else. With their towering shade removed, more sunlight could now reach the ground, making the pathways easier to walk along and also safer. We added green gardens along the public pathway, for both safety and visual benefits. The garden design, a linear landscape slope, completely hides the ventilation void and also helps prevent people from falling into it. While not actually connected to the new mall, the landscape appears as the green plinth, providing pedestrians with a relaxing green sight as they walk past. A series of local shrubs and flowers were strategically planted to create blooming garden throughout the year. Compared to the original hardscape-only design, this new landscape helps to reduce the temperature at ground level, making it much more comfortable to walk. The new sub-drainage system we installed helps to reduce excessive surface runoff water, and limits the chances of flooding. Excess water is collected for irrigation of the plantings.

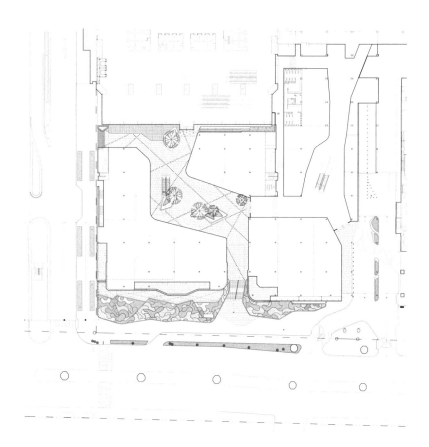

Other than the green landscape, the rest of the area is now designated for pedestrians only. The visually clean hardscape creates a simple and flat walking surface for everyone including the disabled. The pathway is now motorcycle-free, and safer for pedestrians. We retained, where possible, all the existing trees along the street to provide some shade during the hot summer days of Bangkok. Previously, pedestrians used only the skywalk, an elevated pathway below the train tracks, to commute through the neighborhood. This new landscape encourages the pedestrians to come down to the ground and get closer to the garden. This way, we believe they could have a better connection with nature and the people around them.

Since its completion, the new landscape has become an example of what Bangkok's other footpaths could become. Pedestrians now walk freely and safely throughout the area. Car drivers now have something green to look at, reducing their stresses from bad traffic conditions in the neighborhood. Passersby stop and take photos of the garden to show to friends and families. Once in a while, special events are organized to create more activities for pedestrians. With the help of the client, we were able to do something that has never been done before in Bangkok. Even though this is just a simple design gesture and the area is only a small section of Bangkok's public pathway system, we believe that in order to make big changes, everyone needs to participate. With this project, we challenged our neighbors to start re-thinking of their properties. If everybody collaborates, we believe that we can create a better pedestrian pathway system for everyone in Bangkok.

Botanica Khao Yai

Botanica Khao Yai is located on the edge of Khao Yai, Thailand's most important national rainforest reserve. This reserve inspired Botanica's landscape design to be seen as a link between nature and architecture. The site—an abandoned parcel of agricultural land separated into two main plots—faces a local road at the front and is flanked by a small mountain at the rear boundary line. The front plot comprises the project's residential area, while the rear plot is reserved as a public park for the recreational activities of the residents and visitors. The project's residential architecture is interpreted as the large trees of the nearby forest, while the landscaped areas represent the lush rainforest groundcover.

For the residential plot, we needed to fit all unit requirements into a compact area. "The Residences," a series of residential blocks, are arranged on a landscape platform. Two six-story buildings, called Block A and Block B, are located along the edge between the two land plots. Block B is a simple six-story residential block, while Block A is a bit more complicated: It has a V-shaped layout. One part of the block has units on all six floors, facing the mountain behind. The other part is in the middle of the first plot, elevated four floors from the ground with units only on the top two floors, facing the front of the property. The elevated units are built on gigantic concrete columns, leaving space underneath as a big open void. Along the roadside there are twelve two-story villas with private gardens and pools.

Despite the architecture's modern and geometrical design, we projected a similar atmosphere to that found in Khao Yai. We utilized the various building heights to maximize on the sunlight qualities throughout the project, using these as the main criteria to recreate a forest-like landscape here. The floating units on the tall columns are reminiscent of the gigantic trees in the forest nearby. Each column is about the same size as the trunks of those trees, and the units above represent the forest canopies. The areas underneath represent the conditions under the natural tree canopies. But nature continues to thrive, often despite the lack of sunlight. Imitating this natural condition, topographic green landforms were created in the shaded residential areas. Local ferns, found in the forest, were used to cover the landform, which we called the Fern Hills. Working with the different qualities of sunlight, the landscape solution successfully introduces an artificial "sustainable forest" to help the residents and visitors feel they are immersed in nature.

The main pedestrian circulation of the area is called the "Path." This serpentine path meanders over the Fern Hills, left and right, and up and down across the landscape, enabling residents to choose their own route amid the natural surroundings to their accommodations. More than being just a movement artery, the path is also a recreational area, where residents can exercise or take a leisurely walk and experience direct contact with nature. The path is linked to the public areas such as the lobby, clubhouse, lift hall, and corridors, which are all designed as open-air without the use of air-conditioning; instead, creating a cool and shady environment with large trees. Natural lighting is also integrated into the entire project, and local materials were selected to harmonize the architecture and the landscape; for example, by using locally acquired mountain stone found at the site during the basement's construction.

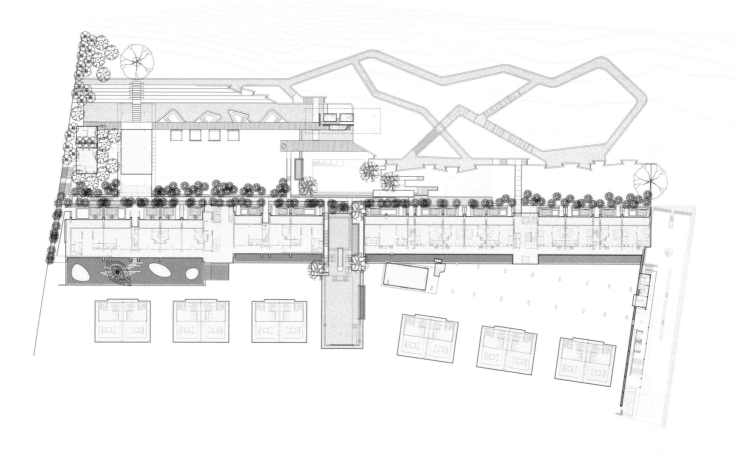

For the site's second (rear) plot, the "Park" was created as the key recreational attraction for all residents and visitors. With the mountain neighboring the boundary line, three layers of subsurface drainage systems were carefully prepared to prevent flooding and protect against landslides. Surplus rainwater is harvested and collected for irrigation during the dry season. A variety of landscape programs were introduced to the property. The Dining Pavilion, hidden by a bamboo forest, is designed to frame the boundary of the park. At the base of the mountain, a green hill is integrated into a reflecting pond, demonstrating the contrast between the artificial and natural landscapes—yet, with the reflection of the mountain, it unites both together seamlessly.

Encouraging the good health was one of our main objectives when designing the residential landscape. Two swimming pools are included in the design: The first pool is located on top of a gym and a lounge. Its reflective water camouflages the massive structure underneath, making it totally disappear. The second pool is in the middle of the park; its water also reflects the mountainous and architectural surroundings, combining all together as part of the overall landscape. A jogging track runs along one side of the park. Trying to achieve the maximum length of the running track, an elevated jogging bridge is introduced as a tool to multiply the routing options for the runners. The bridge shape also echoes the mountainous skyline of the surrounding area.

Overall, we have developed designs within a contemporary context, but we've kept intact the essence of a tropical feeling and atmosphere. This was achieved through the careful consideration of the appropriate layout to ensure the residents can see the beautiful panoramic views of Khao Yai. We believe that contemporary design does not have to be in opposition to nature. The intention for the concept was to create the friendly "forest" to reduce the harshness of a manmade structural form, thus merging the building and surrounding nature into one.

BOTANICA KHAO YAI

Jing'An Century

As the only connection between the pedestrian paths and the sales office, the landscape design of Yanlord's Jing'An Century catalyzes an experience of wandering in nature. The site, a sales gallery for Yanlord Jing'An, is located in one of Shanghai's core central districts and will be developed into residential apartments surrounded by cultural institutions, offices, and commercial developments. The landscape area is not large (only 30-by-20-meters) and is situated right next to busy streets with no natural scenery around. To transform the small yet fully exposed space, our landscape design draws inspiration from the classical Chinese garden to create the illusion of a larger and greener space with layered plantings and a reflective water feature. Our design team believes that landscape design should complement the architecture and its context. Natural elements—like forest, river, and light—were presented, fitting with the urban aesthetic to celebrate the architecture and to evoke a sense of peace and pleasure.

As the site is relatively compressed and starved for green space, this design leverages its constraints and inspiration to lead to four stages of a visiting experience. Much attention was initially given to fostering a strong yet dynamic connection between the building and its landscape, optimizing the layers of curved planters, and composing forced perspectives. Visitors are guided to walk through the choreographed landscape sceneries before entering the sales gallery. The purpose of the opening stage, the arrival, is to define a setting to celebrate the architecture. To make a compatible impression, we expanded the architectural visual language by applying a similar material to the feature wall along the public walkway. Two featured walls following the sidewalk leak an opening to bring spatial fluidity to this area as a whole. Thus, the arrival experience not only offers a sense of urban context from the street but also forecasts a surprise factor within the courtyard.

JING'AN CENTURY

The second experience, the journey, aims to add a representation of mother nature for long-term benefit. By leveraging landform, the design creates a multidimensional volume of greeneries in this limited space and facilitates the feeling of being in a forest wonderland. As visitors walk into the forest court, they can feel a softer and more relaxed environment with a simple and elegant taste. The planting at the entrance announces the opening and guides people through a meandering waterscape. Moving over halfway, the courtyard is lightened up by the water reflection engaging visitors to take a closer look at the courtyard. At the end of the forest court, the ornamental garden, the landscape of sense, immerses the visitor in the beauty of the landscape and creates an illusion of urban escape. With recycled gravel floor and well-composed perspectives, the visitor becomes aware of the crunching walk underneath, the sound of gurgling water, and the misty forest from afar. Together, the orchestration of light, water, and texture fill the space with peace and mystery.

On the west side of the meeting room, we created a sloped terrain to fence off the parking lot. Here, our aim was to create a space whereby the visitor feels enclosed by nature. By adding broadleaf plants like Alocasia and Blue Ice Cypress, the design team played with different tones of greens to enhance the comforting effect through the outdoor scenery. When chatting in the meeting room, one can get a real sense of nature as the Chinese Tallow trees cast their shimmering shadows on the carpet.

Within a busy district of Shanghai, we transformed a small lot into a spectacular urban escape, a journey through nature—forest, water, and light. A fitting compliment to the classical Chinese garden, Jing'An Century presents the illusion of a larger space, a peaceful place where the visitor feels ensconsed in nature.

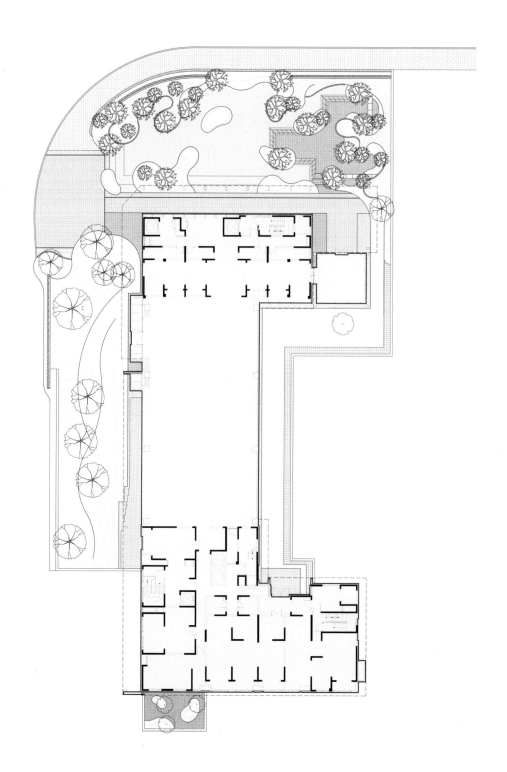

Pyne by Sansiri

Our firm was commissioned to design a garden for Pyne by Sansiri, a high-end condominium. Located right in the middle of Bangkok's busy urban district, just a 5-minute walk from the biggest shopping malls, the site is also next to the BTS (Bangkok's Sky Train) station. Although the location was superb from a commercial perspective, it was not a perfect site for living. Surrounded by three sides of buildings, including noisy nightclubs, even the convenient presence of the train station made the whole space look crowded. Our challenge was to create a pleasant livable environment for the residents, using landscape as the tool for a better quality of life for the city's next generation.

The new building was trapped tightly among the surrounding buildings, and so our main task was to separate the project from its neighbors. To create a private space, separated from the busy outside world, we built a 3-meter-tall wall with planters on the top. From the outside, the wall appears like a normal straight white marble wall, but, looking from inside, the wall is changed into a curvy line to get rid of the boxy feeling space. We strategically located a green area behind the wall, in between the train station and the condominium. Rather than employ a typical functional garden, we planted an urban forest, with 10-meter-tall trees, to reduce the impact of the nearby station. Underneath the trees, our design team installed a series of small green "hills" all the way along from the boundary wall right next to the lobby. To maximize the soft surface, the hills undulate, so the residents can see more greenery than just a flat garden.

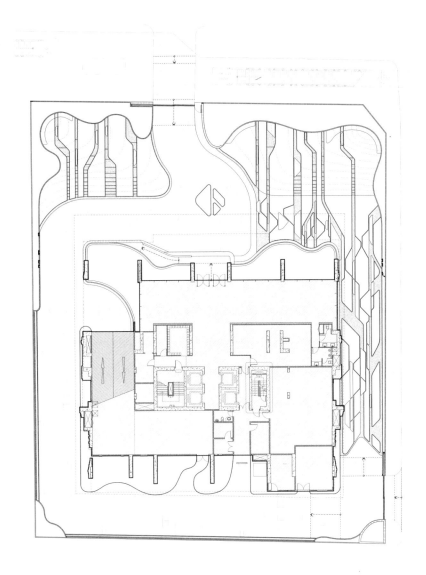

We avoided perpendicular lines in this project, and instead employed angled ones with round corners. Steps are integrated into the hills for an easier walk, dividing the hills into topographic patterns. To animate the forest, we designed some special sculptures, the Dearest Deers, as the inhabitants of the forest. On the flat area, a series of concrete pathways are orchestrated from one side of the property to the other. The contrast between green lawn and concrete paths creates a delightful visual for the residents who live above.

The residential tower is constructed on top of the building's parking structure. As the parking area has a bigger floor plan than the residential area, the leftover area is usually used to house the condominium's swimming pool. Named The Pool @ Pyne by Sansiri, this is exactly the case, and here on the roof of the parking area, on the eighth floor. In order to get rid of that boxy feeling, our first move was to create a "loose" floor plan. Instead of a typical rectangular pool deck, we proposed a series of smaller terraces integrated with the swimming pool. A series of green planters were also inserted here and there, combining all three elements—water, terraces, and plantings—seamlessly.

Most pools in Bangkok located on the roof top are called "Sky Pool." While at first their novelty caused excitement, it soon wore off. Our task therefore was to design not only an attractive swimming pool but one with a unique landscape feature with a character with which the residents could identify. In an effort to make this pool different to other rooftop pools, we framed the swimming pool three-dimensionally with a light cladded structure we nicknamed the "Skeleton." In this way, passersby below would be able to recognize the presence of the pool, and the pool is now fully integrated into the architecture of the building. Not only are the swimmers able to enjoy the spectacular view afforded by the pool, but the BTS passengers can look up and see the special space inside the frame. At night, the "Skeleton" glows, giving the architecture some lightness it so badly needed in its crowded surroundings.

PYNE BY SANSIRI

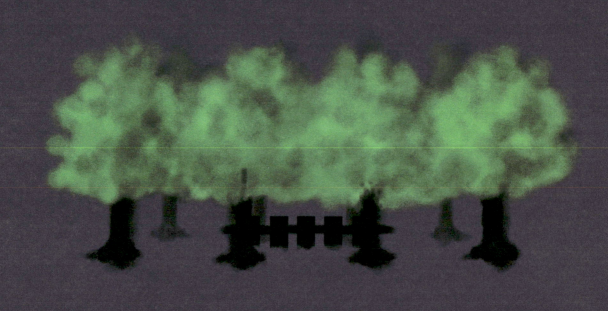

J Residence

This private garden, designed for a successful businessman, enjoys a tranquil setting next to an old golf course on the outskirts of Bangkok. The garden encompasses traditional Thai ideas, creating a beautiful setting that also provides edible plants. The green space was created to be an extension of the house, comprising a series of "Garden Rooms." Here the owner could invite his friends to visit and enjoy the facilities.

The landscape setting on this 1.5-acre plot evokes peace, providing the perfect place for the owner to relax and also to entertain friends. We devised a master plan that would address the needs of the owner from the very moment he arrived home. The strategically purposed set of "Garden Rooms" that serve different functions throughout the day begins with the Arrival Court. When the owner returns after work or from his travels, he is welcomed home with a clean and simple courtyard, right in front of his doorstep. The road surface is kept to a minimum, just enough to connect the Arrival Court and the parking lots.

Two major landscape elements, the Tree Gallery and the Main Axis Corridor, function as circulation backbones, enticingly leading the owner and his guests to different parts of the garden. One may be drawn to the edge of the property to the pergola positioned within its watery setting, or perhaps enticed to walk along the boardwalk, enjoying the sound of trickling water along the rock pool or finding one's gaze drawn toward a feature element, such as an imposing ceramic pot framed by a wooden arbor with creeping plants hanging down.

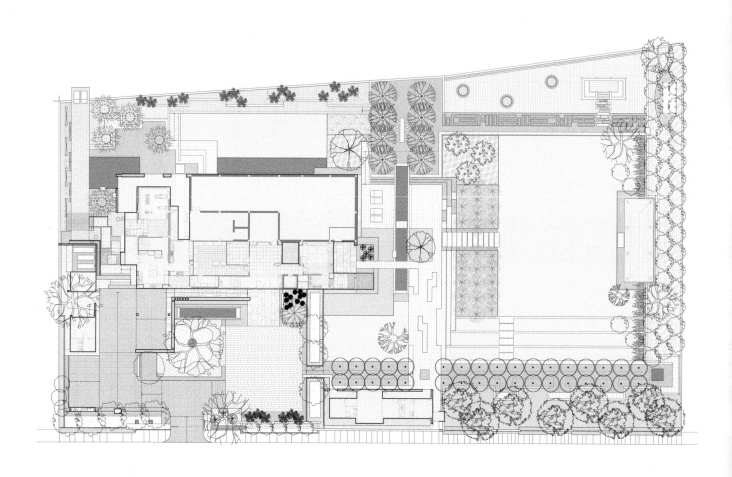

TROP terrains + open space

Each "Garden Room" is attached to the main circulation corridors. As an extension of the main house, they each offer differing purposes, such as a function room, a party room, a play room, a sitting room, a reading room and a dining room, and so on. But these outdoor spaces are composed of living elements: groundcovers, shrubs, hedges, and trees. Without any concrete barriers, the breeze wafts through the garden, providing a refreshing touch. The ceilings of these external spaces consist of green canopies, allowing the sunlight to permeate while also providing cooling shade. Outdoor seating under large established trees creates a wonderful area for al fresco dining. For inclement weather, additional seating is set beneath a large wooden pergola.

Since ancient times, Thai gardens were created to be productive, providing edible plants and herbs. A traditional Thai garden is known as "Pak Suan Krua," literally translating as "kitchen garden." This same concept was applied to the garden at J Residence, but the productive garden here hides in plain view, and appears at first glance to be just like an English garden. Pathways are set amid fruit trees. The old golf course provides a verdant background with pleasant scenery. To maximize the potential of the garden, the design team strategically blurred the borderline. Instead of establishing a boundary to separate the garden from its surroundings, they proposed a Reflecting Pond at the edge to integrate the garden with the neighboring golf course, resulting in spectacular views. The garden design succeeds in bringing all the areas together, drawing the visitor in to explore and allowing the owner to share his tranquil setting with friends.

Ad Lib

In a crowded neighborhood of Bangkok, our client had a vision to convert his abandoned townhomes into a new long-stay hotel to cater for international clientele and their families who were seeking treatment at the neighboring hospital. Located in a small dead-end alley, the potential site offered no views for the residents. Instead, our team focused on creating a garden that would reduce the temperature of the site and focused on an extant enormous tree right in front of the property's wall to provide a viewpoint. Happily, the large mature tree, a *Ficus Benjamina Linn*, was a substantial size and became the main feature of the new hotel complex. From everywhere within the property, this wonderful tree would be visible. As Thai people generally do not plant a Ficus tree at their home, preferring instead to have them at temples, this one was most likely the result of an accident. But we were able to convince the team that this magnificent tree, with its beautiful branches and large hairy roots, was a critical feature for the landscape design.

The site was compact, with the abandoned townhomes on both sides facing each other. The buildings needed to be retained, and transformed into hotel rooms, with windows looking right at the drop-off area. The new lobby and restaurant were slated to be built between the two structures, making the site even more crowded. Our primary goal was to create a space with comfortable living conditions for hotel residents by actively reducing the overall site's temperature by a few degrees. This would create a tranquil and cool place for the residents, one that would function as a second home for the weeks or even months of their stay.

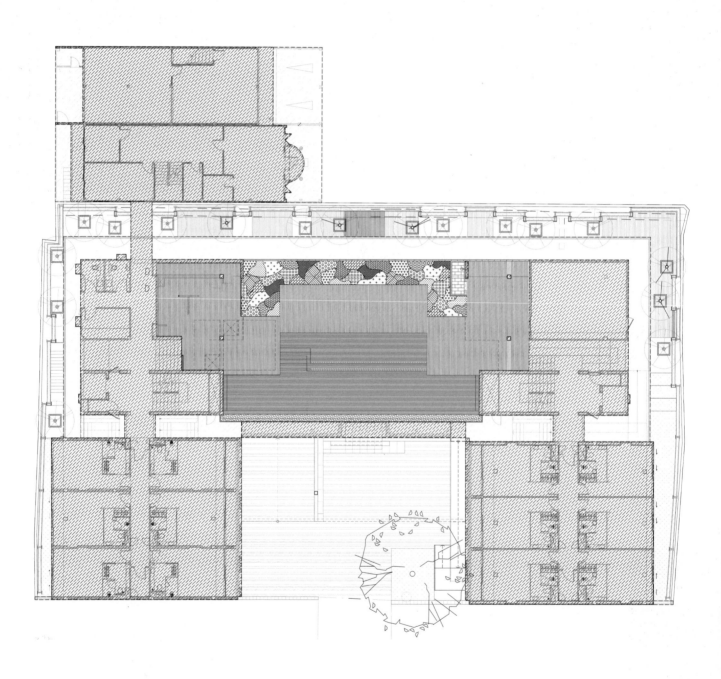

The shade provided by the enormous tree was a decided bonus in our plan, and well-worth any extra complication in construction around it. Additionally, the Thai phrase "Rom Pho Rom Sai" (literally: "under the ficus shade") carried the added meaning of someone who protects and offers safety. The tree provides not only a focal point, but a different visual texture from the surrounding buildings and other greenery. But including the large tree was not enough. We strategically replaced old concrete walls with beautiful tall green walls, adding verdancy to the site. We installed a series of stacked planters, watered by a drip irrigation system to reduce water consumption, and planted *Epipremnum aureum* (commonly known as Devil's Ivy) in them. These beautiful green façades with their long, trailing stems are visible from inside the restaurant, resulting in a pleasing view rather than oppressive concrete walls. It also meant that the guests could sit outside in comfort, as the green wall significantly reduces the heat.

We planted a beautiful Thai herb, *Thunbergia laurifolia Lindl*, outside the windows. This fast-growing tropical vine with its delightful flowers covered most of the windows within months, acting as a living curtain to filter outside heat from entering the rooms. We placed a swimming pool on top of the restaurant's roof. Not only does the pool provide a place to relax and soak up the sun, the water in the pool acts as insulation, helping to reduce the heat for the diners below. While relaxing, the swimmers enjoy a view of downtown Bangkok against a backdrop of verdant greenery. Sympathetic construction works in tandem with the planting scheme to provide a beautiful and tranquil hidden oasis, to the surprise visitors who are amazed to find this tropical paradise right in the middle of a busy Bangkok neighborhood.

Quattro by Sansiri

In a sign of the times, Bangkok is increasingly turning to vertical living options to house residents. Quattro is a high-end residential condominium situated in the upscale area of Bangkok. The proposed site for the structure was an old house with a large garden. On our first visit, we noticed beautiful and mature raintrees (*Leguminosae mimosoideae*), and decided that these must be saved. We worked closely with the owners, the architects, and legal consultants in order to preserve the trees, and eventually it was agreed to locate the residential towers away from the existing raintrees. We were able to persuade the developers that this existing greenery was a priceless feature, and should be retained for the benefit of the existing inhabitants (squirrels and birds) but also for the future benefit of the new residents. These trees became the heart of our design, and we worked to create the other garden elements to complement them.

With the trees now as the main feature of the garden design, we set out to create an urban oasis right in the middle of the city. We began studying these fabulous raintrees, and noting all the effects they had on the surrounding area, such as filtering sunlight through their leaves, creating a more comfortable temperature under their canopies. We decided to locate our proposed seating pavilions under their sheltering branches. But in order to minimize any negative impact to their roots, we avoided using hardscape methods and instead implemented a series of softscape terraces, planted with Mouse Tail Plant (*Phyllanthus myrtifolius moon*), and small pebbles in between, creating a microclimate effect. We were also careful to position the main pool away from the root balls. Placed by the boundary wall, and raised at approximately 80 centimeters from the garden, the infinity edge and its over-flowing water creates a white noise effect that helps to reduce the outside traffic noises.

QUATTRO BY SANSIRI

Design-wise, we took inspiration from the project's name, Quattro (4). So we played with a combination of rectangular shapes, combining them into three-dimensional garden compositions. Some bigger rectangles become terraces, while the smaller ones are used as stepping pathways. A series of rectangular stones is also used on the pavilions' walls, creating semi-enclosed space for their users. We want the Main Garden to be a memento of the former garden and the old out-of-town houses. A big open space with nothing in between the ground and the sky, except the raintrees' huge canopies. A rarity for this kind of project.

In line with the increase of high-rise living, we wanted to accommodate this tendency by creating two small roof gardens. Tower A had a pool terrace on its roof, providing an incentive for residents to live in the tower and also providing insulation to reduce heat for the units underneath. Without much space for a garden, we elected to use two frangipani (*Plumeria rubra*) trees that would extend over the water, and the shade would help reduce the glare that might be reflected into the surrounding units.

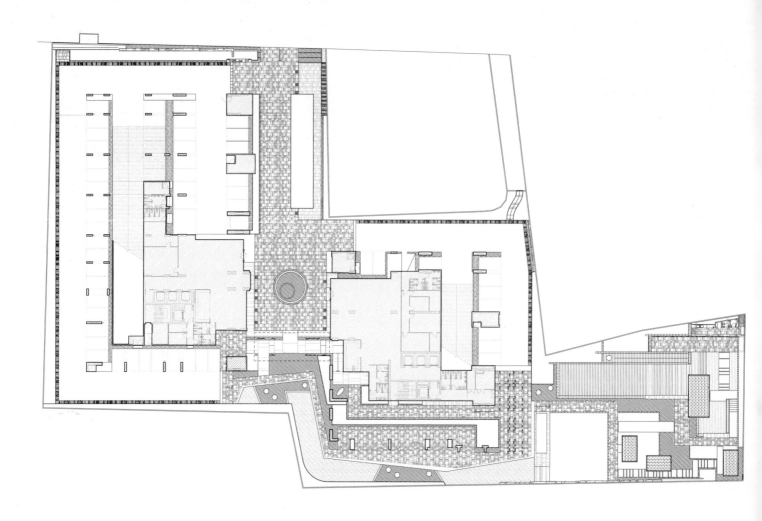

Tower B did not require another swimming pool, being so close to the one situated in the Main Garden. So for its roof garden we decided to design a terrace that could be used for multipurpose activities, a Party Terrace. We divided the space into two small hardscape areas, and placed a reflecting pond in between. We used local Bangkok trees, Indian oak (*Barringtonia acutangula*) and Pong Pong Tree (*Cerbera odollam gaertn*) to create a cool microclimate, allowing the terrace to be used all day, despite the heat. The residents at Quattro are often living in apartments with three generations of the family in one household. What we wanted to create for these people here is not just any garden but a special place. A place where they can spend the rest of their lives. A place where the elders can have their own comfortable space. A place where children can be raised. A true urban oasis for all three generations.

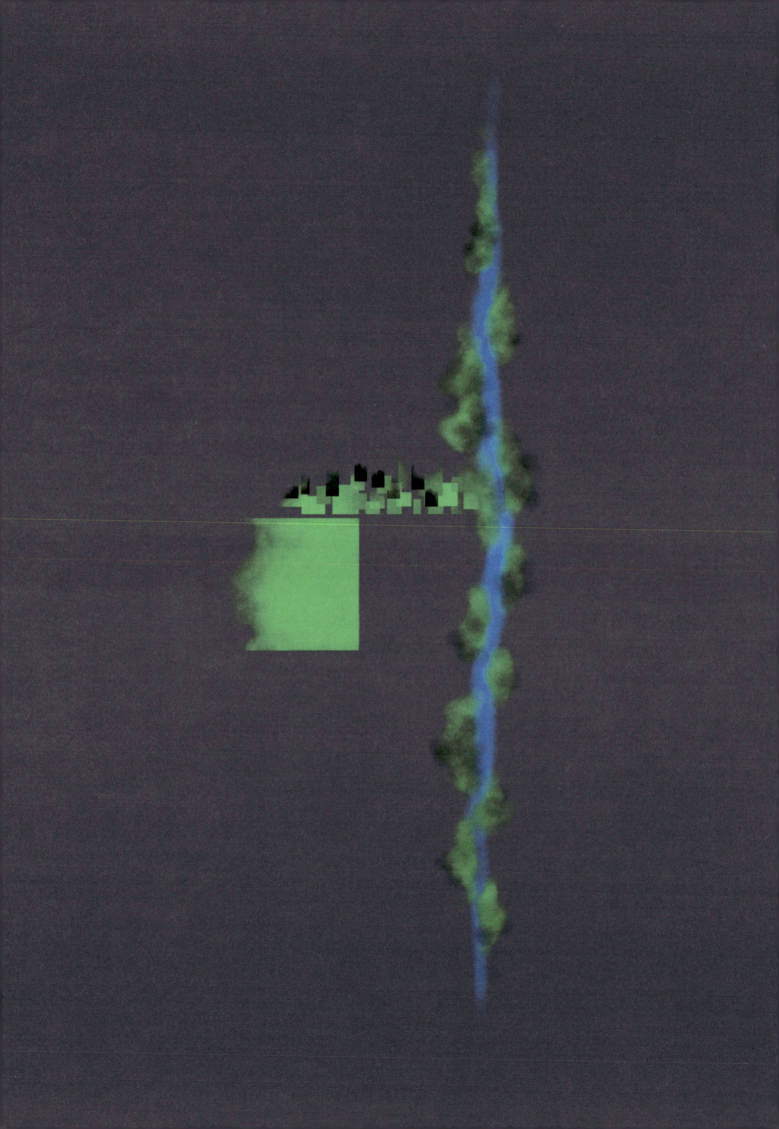

Urban Green Valley

With this site (also known as Yanlord Arcadia) positioned in the center of Shanghai, we wanted to create a public commercial district that differs from the traditional, fully enclosed community. This commercial district connects the site with Jiangpu Park directly to the south with the riverside greenbelt to the east, providing residents and the public with many opportunities to explore an urban "green valley" with an integrated boundary within these surroundings. In China, historically, commercial projects provided only enough space for shops and advertising boards, often abandoning suitable outdoor space for trees or landscaping, citing they'd block views or opportunities to promote businesses. These days, however, multimedia diversification has enabled a different shopping or business experience—one that does not depend significantly on random passersby. Furthermore, the improvement in living standards has enhanced people's demand for quality outdoor space. The traditional, large, hardscape plaza no longer attracts and retains visitors. Thus, we aimed for a place that first would suit people's various forms of activities, which would then lead them to stay and enjoy the commercial value of the surrounding district.

In the overall planning and positioning, we connected to Jiangpu Park on the south side and the riverside walkway on the east—forming a beneficial green space for visitors to stroll through and enjoy, at the same time driving the commercial vitality of the entire riverside area into a community retail street. Our landscape design inherited the design language that is consistent with the architectural design. The commercial space is designed as an emotional experience brought on by nature. It subverts the traditional and rigid large-scale commercial block form and creates an immersive forest-like green valley "commercial" experience by means of natural, mixed planting. The scale of the design touches on the region's historic references to a traditional Shanghai laneway, but here our focus is to create a unique take on this open, three-dimensional green community commercial block. Our landscape design language is extracted from the architecture, so by integrating the landscape and the architecture into the concept of an urban green valley, the entire space retains an active business atmosphere.

URBAN GREEN VALLEY

We went beyond the traditional tree canopy motif and maximized the greening areas by planting on different floor levels, creating a three-dimensional forest. We continued the layered appearance of the buildings by humanizing the scale piece by piece, making each aspect a reduced version of the landscape elements to derive various beautiful and chic leisure spaces. We adjusted what were direct fire access passages into curves, so that the greenery surrounding the passages is staggered, effectively "raising the green volume" to create the effect of space wrapped in greenery. The completed elevated platform is also wrapped in greenery, providing a strong green visual impact from any viewpoint, allowing pedestrians to be seen walking through the site just as if they are in a forest. The urban furniture is a barrier-free, light, and suspended bench. Different heights formed through the folding of the floor coverings satisfy the different scale needs of adults and children. We designed a delightful waterscape that extends to project entrance, making the circulating water a three-dimensional and layered art installation, retaining the focus of sight on all sides. In order to continue the texture of the original lane, both sides of the entrance are deliberately narrowed to form the street life space of old Shanghai; under the green decoration, it is filled with a memorable and lively atmosphere.

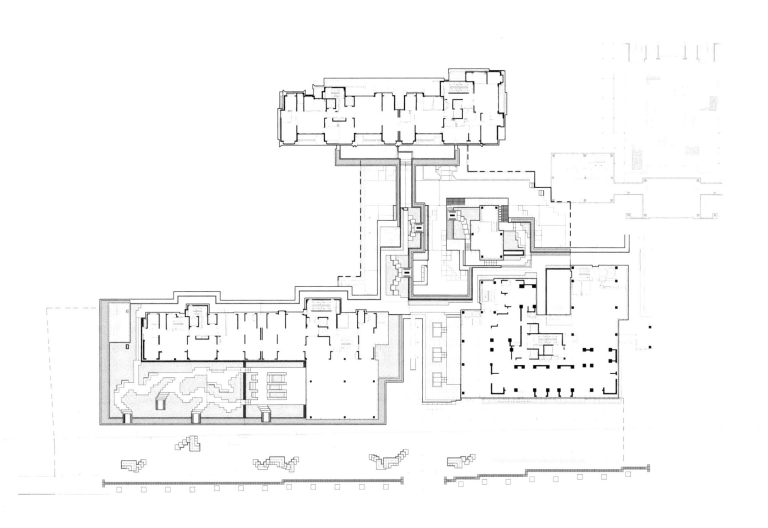

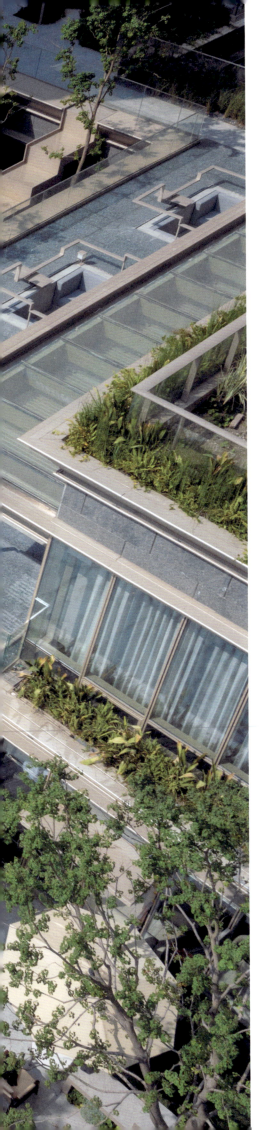

The second level of the exhibition center features a garden shared by the district's residents. The design combines the bookstore functions of the exhibition center as well as accommodates the needs of the community gym and residents. The garden is divided into two areas: the private and relatively public. The side that is closest to the bookstore is the public reading space, allowing users to read books while appreciating the winding and green small-scale forest. At the end of the forest is a little square where small-scale activities can be organized, including space under the tree shade for outdoor yoga. On the other side of the garden is a private garden that allows residents to enjoy a close interaction with the natural world. Here, residents can experience the charm of seasonal plants to alleviate the stresses of city life. There are four exquisitely designed and carefully positioned cantilever platforms that protrude unwittingly as a quiet invitation to people to visit Jiangpu Park and other Shanghai landmarks. The west platform and the lantern-like landscape corridor are combined to indicate the start of the site experience. Also on the second level is a bar seating area in the water, a highlight and feature of the project. It includes two main design details: its safety railings are decorated with special light strips that act as a precaution against accidental falls into the water, and three rotating dining tables under the special light strips meet the functions of outdoor dining and partying.

As a final note, planting also creates "places." Our design pays significant attention to the overall mood of the plants rather than the display of design per se, by focusing on the stable ecological lifecycle of plant relationships. Following the rule of competition in nature, the plants are allowed to grow freely, to infiltrate, to intermingle, to reach a harmonious and natural state of growth that conveys the beauty of cyclical plant life changes. Both the natural and urban landscapes will continue to grow and flourish naturally through the seasons, allowing people to appreciate the thrilling beauty of nature, which bestows an inner joy.

Ashton Residence 41

Situated in Sukhumvit, a prime but dense neighborhood in Bangkok, this project is a high-end low-rise condominium. It is similar to other new condominiums in this area of the city, as the available plots of land are limited. As such, the available area for our landscape design was reduced to a channel-like narrow space located in between the twin main buildings. And, of course, the façades. The two buildings were built to a mirror plan, meaning that they each face the neighboring building on the opposite side. The balconies were tilted to an angle of 45 degrees as a way of slightly turning them away from facing directly across the channel.

We were able to introduce a planting scheme In between each balcony, creating tall, vertical greenery that extends from the ground floor almost to the roof, engendering distinct rhythms between the built structure and nature. These green walls provide a welcome sight of plant life, giving the residents something green to catch their eye without filling the balconies with potted plants. In addition, these living curtains help to absorb the heats while also catching dust and providing more oxygen, creating a pleasant microclimate.

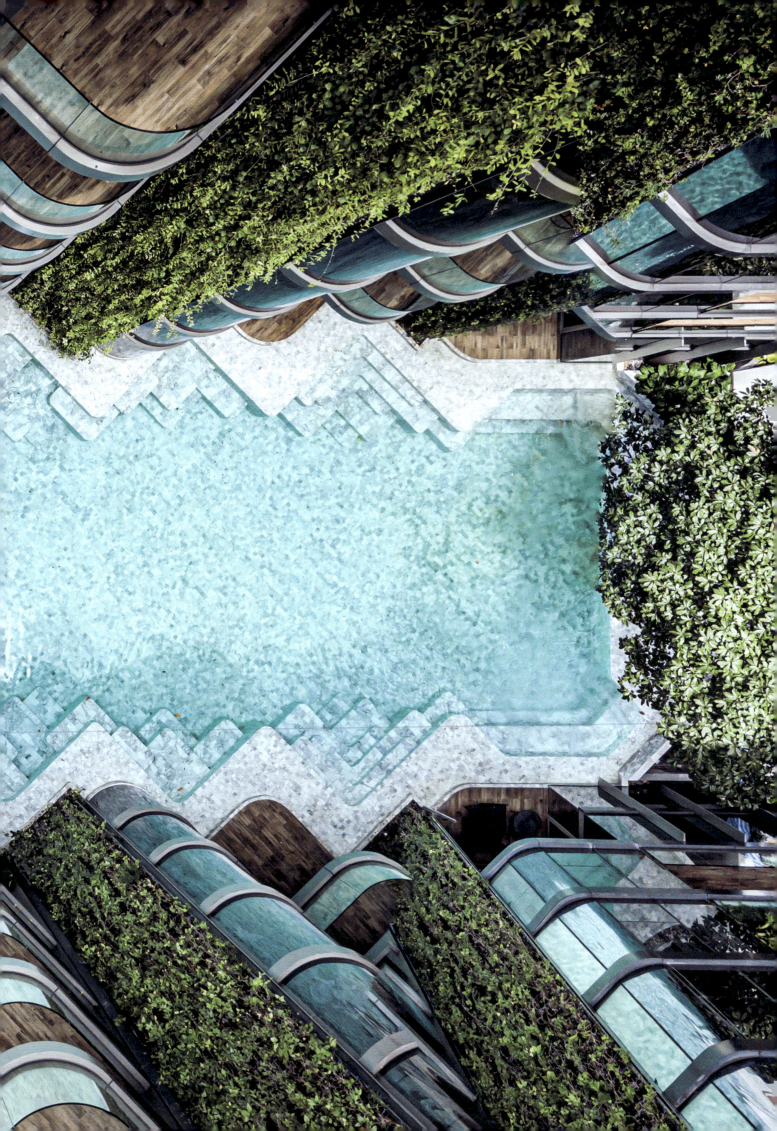

We placed the main pool for the condominium in the narrow area between the two buildings. Looking down from the balcony, the pool with its light-blue color set amid the light-colored stone surrounds offers a wonderful glimpse of tranquil repose. Our team wanted to view the twin buildings as forming a gorge, with the pool acting as a creek in the valley channeling between the two sides. The underwater seating and stairs of the pool are designed to imitate a rocky stream place, offering a place where people may rest after a dip in the creek. To establish privacy around the pool, we employed levels at the ground floor to divide the semipublic space comprising the car drop-off point and the main entrance with that of the pool area.

Each building is endowed with a roof garden. We planned for these gardens to function as a catchment for rain water and also to reduce the overall heat gain. As some residents have direct access to the roof from their apartments, we had to ensure that our design maintained a proper sense of privacy for them. We added various rooms and corners with seating to create privacy but still open to the outside for the views. Raised planter beds are employed to define private space, and are located between the seating and the circulation.

With the addition of vertical greenery and the careful positioning of roof gardens on the two buildings, our design brings a welcome sight of green for the residents and passersby while also ensuring privacy for the inhabitants of Ashton Residence 41.

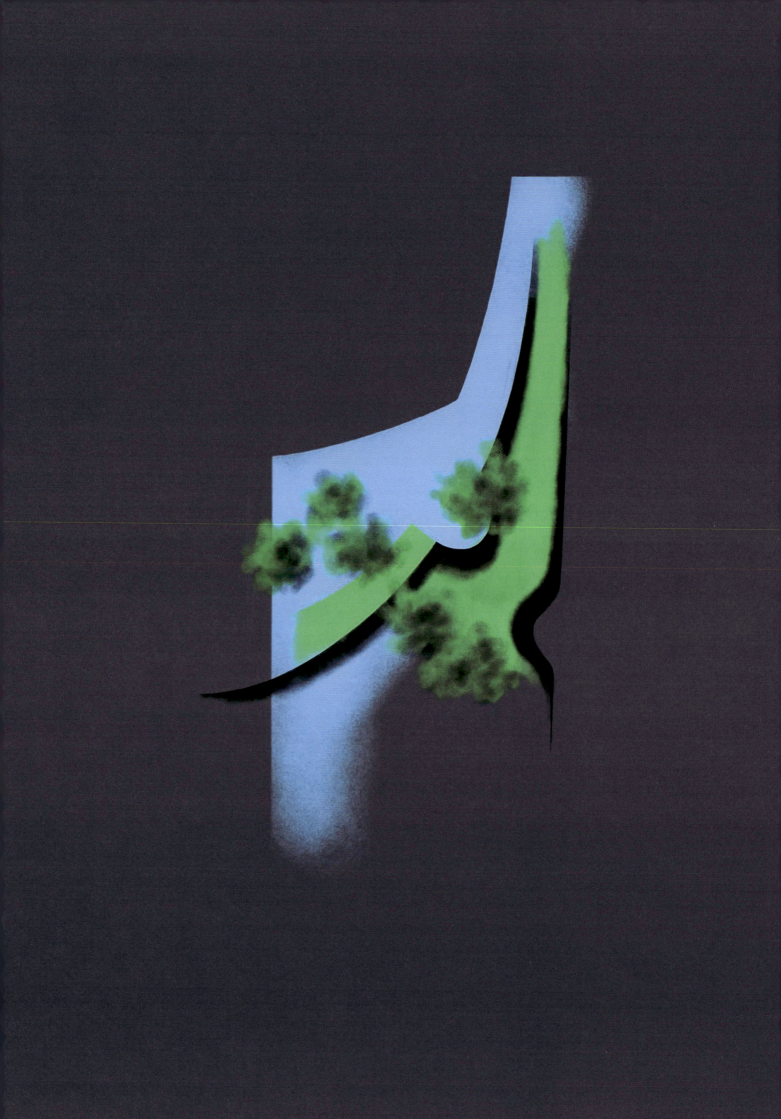

Hilton Pattaya

For this project, we sought to create an urban sanctuary, hidden from the chaos of the noisy beach below. Located in Pattaya (a two-hour drive from Bangkok), the building is set across from a famous, beautiful long beach, with an unobstructed sea view. The beach has over the years become crowded with nightclubs and bars catering to the tourists. The Hilton Pattaya, with 200 rooms, is built on the roof of a new shopping center. This rooftop site came with limitations of space, but our design team was determined to overcome any problems in order to connect the hotel with the beautiful sea view while also providing a serene environment for the guests staying at the Hilton Pattaya.

Our brief included not only the Hotel Garden, located on the 16th floor, but also the Hotel drop-off area, on the ground floor. On our first visit to the site, we noticed three important things that would affect the design greatly. Firstly, the shopping center roof included a skylight, but, structurally, we determined that it could not support any additional loading so could not be included in our design. In addition, the mall did not possess extra funds for decoration so it remains as it was built with half glass and half concrete.

Further, the skylight was positioned right in the middle of the shopping mall roof, leaving us with only small and narrow areas around it for our garden design. The limited space necessitated the removal to other areas of the gym, toilets, a fire-exit staircase, and M&E rooms. The roof of the mall has an irregular edge, due to its in and out façade. Thus, these in and out areas and edges had a big impact on our design. To resolve all these pre-existing issues, we elected to divide the garden into three main components. Firstly, we created a Sand Court for the hotel's lobby on the 16th floor. When the guests step out of the elevators, the first thing they see is our Sand Court, with only two elements: sand and green plants. Sand was selected because of its relationship with the ocean and beach. The Sand Court can be transformed as a piece of canvas for installations throughout the year. Such as red-colored Chinese decorations during the Lunar New Year, or perhaps Christmas ornaments in December.

Our second element was used to strategically maximise the garden area. We created a Sun Deck to sit on top of the gym and toilet roofs, extended and connected to the 17th floor. The result is a reasonable-size deck with direct access from the hotel. Instead of walking through the lobby, guests can walk directly to the pool area. We stipulated that the infinity pool was to be placed at the edge of the roof, making the water visually connected with the ocean below. The pool was designed as one big sheet of water, with the Lap Pool, Fun Pool, Jacuzzi Maze, and Kid Pool all hidden underneath the same water surface. Inspired by a school of shiny fish, we added fiber optic lighting to the bottom of the pool so, at night, it glows just like those silvery fish, creating the same effect as stars.

HILTON PATTAYA

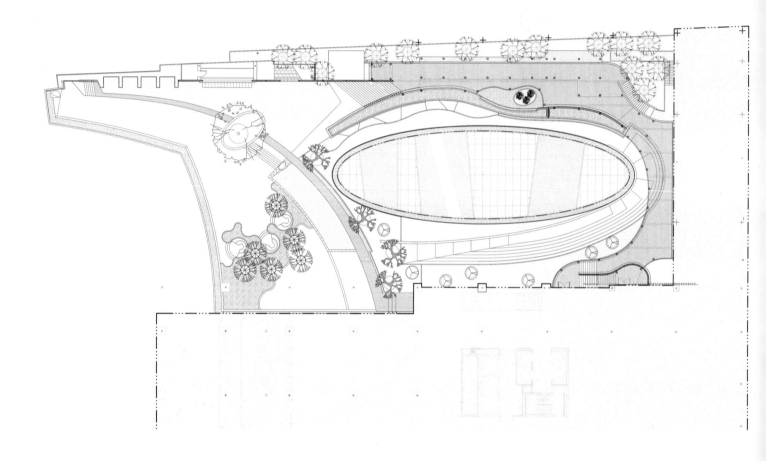

We made the decision to only use indigenous species in our planting scheme, to reference the beach location. Around the skylight for screening purposes, we planted Beach naupaka (*Scaevola taccada Roxb.*), frangipani (*Plumeria aduminata Art.*), and Betel palm trees (*Areca catechu*). Calabash (*Crescentia cujete*) trees used in the Jacuzzi Maze area create a sculptural effect above the water and also provide some shade and privacy for the swimmers. Despite the limited space and the problematic elements we encountered, we succeeded in creating and combining the three components together to create a true hidden sanctuary above Pattaya's Skyline.

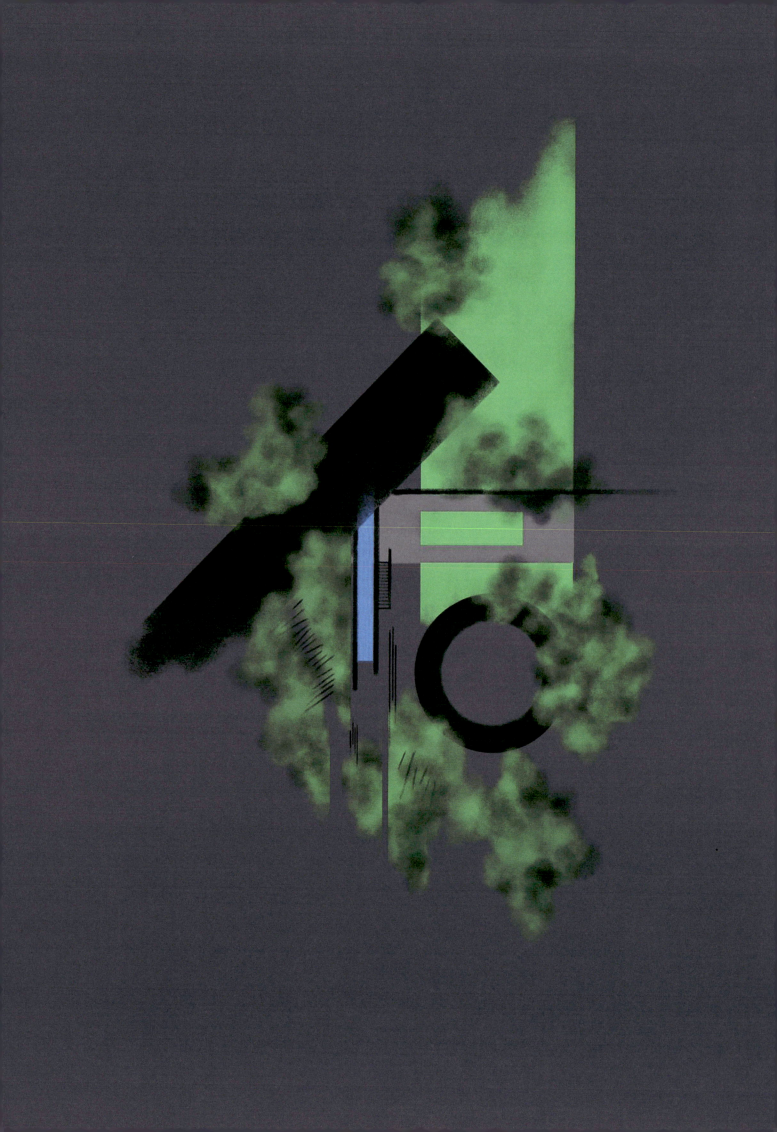

Chiang Rai Residence

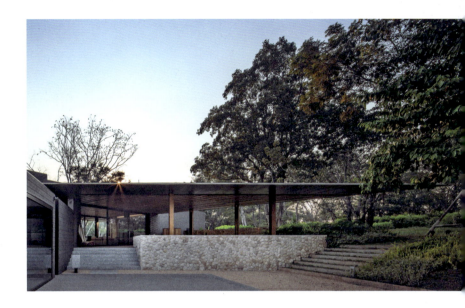

Set in Thailand's northern region, the Chiang Rai Residence project is a composition that merges both the natural setting and architecture into a harmonious space that holds its own independent ownership, while at the same time blending in well with the context of the lives of those who dwell here. The design is both prosaic and aesthetic; yet its overall impression is simple and charming. Upon arrival, the obscurity of the landscape's "form" represents not only the defeat of authorship but also ownership. Neither the house nor its owner owns this landscape. Rather, the landscape is set to be an integral part of the lives it hosts.

From the outside, little if anything of the landscape settings is overtly disclosed. The terrain is leveled and stratified without any legible geometric forms. Everything seems naturally drawn, pushed and pulled together by topographical forces. Instead of accentuating the house, the landscape becomes a mute or rather quiet expression, receding into the leaves of its lush trees. Our first and foremost requirement was to preserve the existing trees in place and protect them throughout the construction process, together in collaboration with the architect, engineers, and client. The trees acted as a pretext to the design, providing the framework for both the house and the landscape. Through the design process, the house and the land gradually merged, becoming a design platform that accepted and welcomed both prosaic and aesthetic transformation. Topographically orchestrated, the levels were carefully matched and integrated with the positioning of layered, stepped terraces, therefore leaving the existing topographic forces uninterrupted, which also resulted in the creation of pleasing and functional forms.

CHIANG RAI RESIDENCE

The landscape of Chiang Rai Residence can also be seen as a network of relationships between the terrain and living. This notion of participation allows the connection between interiority and exteriority, as well as the transition between distinct activities. The connection is both spatial and actual. The terraced landscape becomes the conduit for the occupants to be able to live beyond the walls; meanwhile, the house sustains the sense of flow. The presence of these terraces is not overly apparent; at times, the terraces seem to disappear. Thus, hints are provided at the threshold, but the actual separations are delayed. As a whole, the landscape of Chiang Rai Residence is formless, as if being shaped and reshaped by specific circumstances and situations. We never felt that the place is "designed" for it to have its own distinct identity; rather, it is built as a framework of lives. Here, the task of describing the place becomes clearer. It is to develop vocabularies that will demonstrate how settings that are distinct from one another can also be interconnected. To inhabit the place means to focus on the performances that the separate settings sustain, and to discover similarities between them. Only in this way can the landscape setting be seen to exhibit not just remoteness but familiarity; that is, the typicality of the lives this landscape is intended to nurture.

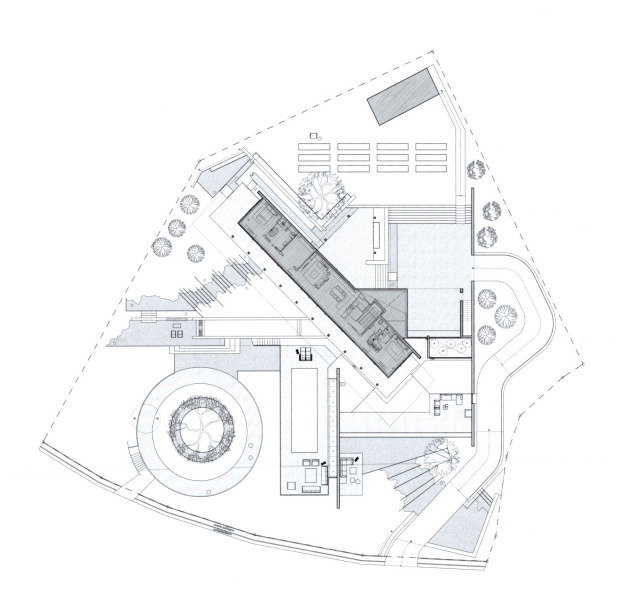

CHIANG RAI RESIDENCE

In terms of site logistics, the region is prone to extreme weather; there's drought in summer and high precipitation in the rainy season, which causes soil erosion. Additionally, the site's terrain contained a low-nutrient soil with a high pH rate. To respond to these challenges and alleviate the extremes, our key strategy was for cost-effective, long-term maintenance of a beautiful and healthy ecosystem. We designed a sustainable planting scheme and topography with minimum disturbance to the site's natural setting. The landscape design interweaves the exterior vertical spaces while paying respect to retain the site's topography as level as possible. We opted for local, hardy, and adaptive planting species that can sustain heavy rainfall, such as Vetiver grass (*Chrysopogon zizanioides*), Fountain grass (*Pennisetum setaceum*), and Minnieroot (*Ruellia tuberosa*). These plants have strong root systems that hold the topsoil and are also drought tolerant. We also planted nitrogen-fixing plants, such as Pinto peanut (*Arachis pintoi*), to improve nutritional deficiencies in the existing soil. The layers of plants and trees create distinctive, picturesque surroundings and sustain their own ecosystems, all the while enabling the beauty of natural change and transformation.

With regards to sustainable water management, our design strategically manages rainfall through different leveling layers of terrain and vegetation. Using gravity, surface water runoff is captured and absorbed by the native and water-tolerant plant species that are dispersed throughout the site. The rain garden is located at the lowest level of the site's terrain to collect and store water during heavy rainfall, and along the slope and hardscape areas, permeable paving materials of local stone and fine gravel allow water to naturally infiltrate the ground.

Ashton Asoke-Rama 9

This project, named after its location at the Rama 9 intersection, was the creation of a new, iconic residential, mixed-use high-rise development. Set in a very busy section of Bangkok, there was very little green space on the existing site. Our team developed a Shared-Green Spaces approach for this design by adding a new public green space to the city. Ashton Asoke Rama 9 therefore helps alleviate the environmental challenges faced by the city while also harmoniously improving living standards for residents and native wildlife.

Our first task was to carefully consider the environmentally sensitive landscape, in an area prone to flooding. We discovered an old canal, long forgotten and disconnected from the canal network. Our team worked with the clients, engineers, and the Bangkok Metropolitan Administration (BMA) to propose the idea of bringing back this disused canal and employing it to collect the stormwater from the project, allowing excess water to be stored during heavy rains and thereby mitigating the risk of flooding. We also altered the overall site base, allowing the landscape to remain at existing grade level and the lower grading level to act as green infrastructure to collect and channel the site's stormwater runoff. We proposed a Green Pause concept to allow the project's stormwater runoff to pause and get treated within the site. The landscape team envisioned this Shared-Green Spaces landscape as a new paradigm of an urban green infrastructure that articulates the theory with aesthetics of landscape design and appropriately applies it to the site context.

For this project, we elected to use a circular form, a shape proven to use less surface area to hold the most amount of water, and also the circle is an abstract form of nature that represents infinity, unity, and harmony. This "O" Plaza is located at the corner of an intersection of the main landscape area. Each circular center is placed to first correlate with the two buildings' axes, which in turn maximizes the circular spaces to create a variety of different-sized outdoor rooms. These rooms are connected with a permeable curved path that continuously traces the circle's periphery.

ASHTON ASOKE-RAMA 9

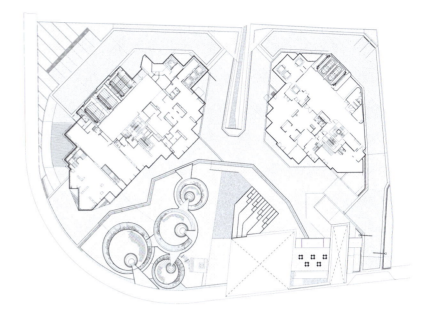

We provided unique "O" seating inside the central space of each room, surrounded by rainforest garden, and set slightly off-center to create privacy and social distancing in the public space. Within each room are steps leading to the ground floor of the rainforest garden, where the visitors can observe the plants and any wildlife while listening to the soothing sounds of the green infrastructure's water cascades.

The "O" Plaza as a landscape space is a new paradigm of an urban green infrastructure articulating theory with aesthetics of landscape design appropriately. Our team integrated water management systems into our design, ensuring that excess water from the installed storage tanks flows to the former canal for storage. Any runoff water from the hardscape flows to the series of water cascades, and as it flows down the steps, any small particles will gravitate to the bottom. At the center of each circular room lies the rainforest garden where water will naturally infiltrate the ground. The landscape team carefully selected native water-tolerant plant materials with high carbon absorption ability such as Indian coral tree (*Erythrina variegata*), Yellow walking iris (*Neomarica longifolia*), and Singapore daisy (*Sphagneticola trilobata*). We created the rainforest garden by combining layers of tree canopies, shrubs, and ground covers to reduce help the city's air and noise pollution.

In addition to the use of green spaces at ground level, we also were able to implement a green roof onto a building setback zone, adding to the Green Stack Gardens throughout inner Bangkok. At the sky lounge, the project offers a floor for each tower for public amenities. As highlighted landscape spaces, infinity-edged double panoramic pools extend out into the sky from the two buildings. To ensure the pool holds something a little extra, we added a sky platform that extends over the pool, out into the air, providing a special feature that offers breathtaking panoramic views and a flexible space that can turn into a stage to facilitate events. Ashton Asoke Rama 9, seen as a prototype of a new urban development, demonstrates the implementation of landscape design's aesthetic and function of green infrastructure to mitigate the city's environmental problems particularly in dense urban areas with the associated challenges and limitations. While it may be viewed as a small-scale landscape intervention, we believe that, expanded and reproduced across the cityscape, together these green urban spaces will have a great impact on our city and be viewed as an efficient tool to enhance the living quality of people and wildlife.

Nana Coffee Roasters Bangna

Located in the large commercial/residential district of Bangna, Nana Coffee Roasters Bangna, in collaboration with Idin Architects, introduces an alternative café design tthat draws visitors away from the buzzing Bangna-Trad motorway, redirecting their focus onto the coffee-drinking experience. Through this concept, the boundaries between three practices—architecture, interior, and landscape—are blurred. This 'blurred' space creates undefined areas where Instagrammable is much less important than the visitor's experience of indulging in a high-quality cup of coffee within the surrounding nature. A series of landscape layers help create a micro-environment for both humans and animals in the area. First, lush greenery protects the property from noise, dust, pollution, and even vibrations from heavy traffic outside.

All existing trees were retained to provide a microclimate, reducing the overall temperature by a few degrees, compared to the surrounding highways and concrete masses. In certain areas, the green landscape was allowed to penetrate into the interior space, while some furniture extended from the interior to each garden terrace, creating an illusion of blending interior and exterior space together. At the same time, this urban sanctuary not only serves human users but also creates biodiversity, with many blooming plant species that provide homes and food for local birds and insects, especially bees and stingless bees.

NANA COFFEE ROASTERS BANGNA

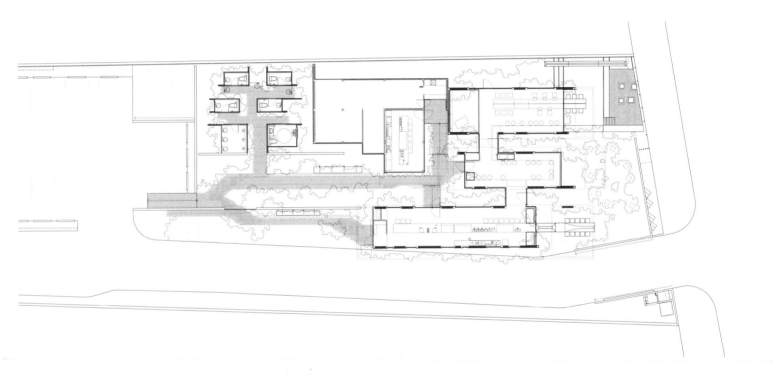

NANA COFFEE ROASTERS BANGNA

Firm Profile

TROP: terrains & open space is an esteemed landscape architectural design studio comprising a dedicated team of 40 talented designers and construction supervisors in Bangkok and Shanghai. Under the visionary leadership of Pok Kobkongsanti, the core philosophy revolves around crafting distinctive designs for each project that TROP works on. TROP firmly believes that the design process is just as integral as the final design itself, and as such, maintains a close, collaborative relationship with all our clients. Pok started his own practice, TROP: terrains & open space in 2007. He named the practice from two of the best tools, terrains, and open space, to create an extraordinary experience for customers. Presently, TROP has garnered an impressive portfolio of projects spanning across Asia with a diverse area of expertise, encompassing Hospitality, Residential, Commercial, Installation design, and Sustainable projects. Pok has an affinity for natural materials, favoring stone, wood, water, light, and sound, this fondness is evident in the firm's unique—yet timeless projects. Apart from the material, Pok also focuses on the experience of the architecture and the landscape as well as concern with the sense of place, where the design must 'belong' to the context.

With more than 20 years of experience, Pok was recently ranked as one of the Top 10 Landscape Architects in the World by the Landscape Architects network. He received 40 under 40 Awards for International Designers by Perspective Magazine, Hong Kong, China.

Additionally, in 2023, The Office of Contemporary Art and Culture, Ministry of Culture of Thailand selected Pok Kobkongsanti as the recipient of The Silpathorn Award, an honor for living Thai contemporary artists who make remarkable contributions to Thai fine arts and culture, in the Architecture category.

Awards

2023
TROP The Silpathorn Award: Living Thai contemporary artists
Urban Green Valley Pro+ Award China: Golden Award—Landscape of the Year
Jing'An Century 9th CREDAWARD: Gold Award—Landscape Design
An Villa DFA Design for Asia Awards: Gold Award

2022
An Villa 8th CREDAWARD: Gold Award—Demonstration Area
An Villa World Architecture Festival: Highly Commended 2022 Landscape Urban
An Villa Architizer A+ Awards: Jury winner—Best Landscape Design Firm

2021
Ribbon Dance Park Architizer A+ Awards: Jury winner—Landscape & Planning—Urban & Masterplans
Chiang Rai Residence Architizer A+ Awards: Finalist—Landscape & Planning—Private Garden

2020
Jing'An Century Pro+ Award China: Golden Award—Landscape of the Year
Botanica Khao Yai German Design Award Winner: Urban scape and infrastructure

2018
Hilton Pattaya TALA Professional Award: Excellence Award
Raintree Residence TALA Professional Award: Excellence Award
Veranda Pattaya TALA Professional Award: Honor Award
Residence Rabbits TALA Professional Award: Honor Award
Botanica Khao Yai TALA Professional Award: Honor Award
Sindhorn Residence TALA Professional Award: Honor Award

2017
Botanica Khao Yai IFLA: Honorable Mention

2016
Groove @ Central World TALA Professional Award: Excellence Award

Baan Plai Haad by Sansiri TALA Professional Award: Honor Award
Ad Lib TALA Professional Award: Honor Award
J Residence TALA Professional Award: Honor Award

2013
Casa de la Flora ASIA Pacific Hotel Awards: Highly Commended—New Small Hotel Construction & Design Thailand

2012
Quattro by Sansiri ASLA: Honor Award in Residential Design
Seascape Sentora Singapore Property Awards: Winner Residential (Low Rise) Category
Hilton Pattaya WAN Awards: Hotel of the Year

2011
Hilton Pattaya Thailand Property Awards: Highly Commended—Best Landscape Architectural Design

Project List

RESIDENTIAL
125 Sathorn, Thailand
28 Chidlom, Thailand
8 Conlay, Malaysia
98 Wireless, Thailand
ARQ10, Thailand
Ascott Thonglor, Thailand
Ashton Asoke, Thailand
Ashton Asoke-Rama 9, Thailand
Ashton Chula- Silom, Thailand
Ashton Residence 41, Thailand
Ashton Silom, Thailand
Avora 31, Thailand
Baan Plai Haad by Sansiri, Thailand
Baan Sansuk by Sansiri, Thailand
Beatniq, Thailand
Cape Royale Sentosa, Singapore
CCH Residence, Thailand
Chapter Chula-Samyan, Thailand
Chiang Rai Residence, Thailand
Dusit D2 Residence, Thailand
Fynn Asoke, Thailand
Haus 23, Thailand
Ideo Q Chula-Samyan, Thailand
J Residence, Thailand
M Phayathai, Thailand
M Silom, Thailand
Noble Around Ari, Thailand
Noble Cube, Thailand
Noble Curate, Thailand
Noble Remix, Thailand
Park Origin Thonglor, Thailand
Pattanakarn Residence, Thailand
Prive by Sansiri, Thailand
Pyne by Sansiri, Thailand
Quattro by Sansiri, Thailand
Raintree Residence, Thailand
Rama IV Residence, Thailand
The Reserve 61 Hideaway, Thailand
The Reserve Sathorn, Thailand
Residence Rabbits, Thailand
RMT 14 Residence, Thailand
S Pavilion, Thailand
Sai Sha, Hong Kong, China
Seascape Sentora, Singapore
Sindhorn Residence, Thailand
Siu Hong, Hong Kong, China
Soonthareeya Ratchadamri, Thailand
The Strand Thonglor, Thailand
Veranda Residence Hua Hin, Thailand
Yanlord Jing'An Century, China
Yanlord on the Park Phase 3, China
Yanlord Qianwan, China
Yanlord The Coast Garden, China
Yanlord The Times Garden, China

COMMERCIAL
72 Courtyard, Thailand
Central Plaza Chonburi, Thailand
Central Plaza Rama 9, Thailand
Groove @ Central World, Thailand
La Vita Sana Khaolak, Thailand
Luxelakes A3, China
Luxelakes A7, China
Museum of Modern Aluminum, Thailand
Nana Coffee Roasters Bangna, Thailand
Zense Gourmet Deck, Thailand

HOSPITALITY
Ad Lib, Thailand
Arom Wongamat, Thailand
Botanica Khao Yai, Thailand
Casa de la Flora, Thailand
Dusit D2 Hotel, Thailand
Hilton Pattaya, Thailand
Karon Hotel, Thailand
La Vela Khaolak, Thailand
Le Meridien Huizhou, China
Veranda Pattaya, Thailand
VERSO Hua Hin—a Veranda Collection, Thailand
Zai, Thailand

MIXED USE & OTHERS
Aman Pavilion, Thailand
An Villa, China
Apac Tower, Thailand
The Center of Universe (Public Art Installation) Thailand
Dadao Century, China
KJL Innovation Campus, Thailand
Life with a View Exhibition, Chiangmai Design Week
Nyx by Sansiri—Sales Gallery, Thailand
Oasis Central Sudirman, Indonesia
Poetic Villa (Yanlord KQ), China
The Reserve Thonglor (Sales Gallery)
Ribbon Dance Park, China
Singha Complex, Thailand
Singha Oasis, Thailand
Sunac Hangzhou, China
Urban Green Valley (Yanlord Arcadia), China
Yanlord Hangzhou—Sales Gallery, China
Yanlord Opus One, China

TROPSTERS

CURRENT: Pok Kobkongsanti, Thansinee Boonjue, Watcharin Changmai, Suphansa Chansanroj, Pakkapong Dechjirakul, Tananya Duangonnam, Guo He, Masukree Hengdada, Kissanapong Hongwanichsakul, Tingting Hu, Nattita Indrasukhsri, Nicharee Jaknoo, Sirinan Junchada, Pranom Khunlao, Piyakan Kleebthong, Romanee Kobkongsanti, Tanutphum Kohkiattrakul, Pin-a-nong La-mor, Warayus Lakpeat, Pinmanee Lamor, Rahut Lertsopaporn, Heidi Liu, Yiping Liu, Yuting Lu, Pattaratida Mahaprom, Hasuwan Mamah, Navapol Montong, Chidsupang Moolfaeng, Maytinee Nakprasert, Darika Nuangboonma, Chanikarn Phitphisarn, Phorames Phorama, Kampon Prakobsajjakul, Jetnipat Prutpaisan, Fusang Ren, Hui Ren, Pengtao Sang, Thongchai Sinsansiri, Nattawat Sirisuwan, Kanjanich Sukrojana, Khanapol Suvarnasuddhi, Panpassa Tawwiset, Thiprath Ubonphaisal, Wei Wang, Nuttaporn Wattanajaroenpoka, Patipan Worawanich, Huamei Yin, Jialuo Yu, Ziyang Yu, Kehan Zhou, Jayda Zhu

PAST: Karin Anukulyudhathon, Bun Asai, Chonfun Atichat, Chatchawan Banjongsiri, Nuttakarn Bunchuensuk, Naratip Bundi, Piyaporn Chaimungkhun, Bumrungpong Chainarapipat, Kunlasatree Chanmuang, Visarut Chantalapho, Krit Chantapireepun, Chanatip Cheevamongkol, Anuwit Cheewarattanaporn, Chawan Chevarunotai, Akachai Choochaiwuttipong, Nakakamol Chueathue, Yuan Fang, Boonsiri Fuekfon, Nutaphol Horthong, Kawinwarong Ingadhamrong, Jirachai Itthisuriya, Sophanut Jamonnak, Pattarapol Jormkhanngen, Chanyarat Karoon-ngampun, Montarat Kasemsuvan, Kittinai Kittirojana, Sorakom Klongvessa, Saranya Leeyakul, Pradit Lertsakul, Yichiao Lin, Siyi Lu, Pitchayut Luadsoongnern, Ke Ma, Thanakorn Malimat, Ekitsara Meedet, Napassorn Methasuraruk, Wasin Muneepeerakul, Worakarn Nakngam, Worrapicha Noree, Pornuma Nualmusik, Tula Nukfon, Supichaya Osothsilp, Mathee Padpai, Nattima Pakdee, Tatsaneeya Pasuk, Sutthiphat Phujeenaphan, Sahaphoom Pitiboriboon, Napatr Pornvisawaraksakul, Supakorn Praditlertsakul, Thitima Prarasre, Nattapong Raktai, Natcha Rungcharoenluk, Jariya Rungsaeng, Nawinda Rungsmai, Peerasit Saengwanloy, Roypim Sakunchareonkij, Theerapong Sanguansripisut, Hatsakarn Senangam, Ibraheng Senlaeh, Piyanat Songkhroh, Yanisa Songserm, Kittinan Sookpan, Sornketrat Sornkamron, Nina Srisamarn, Boontarika Suwanteepratch, Yunya Tang, Tanakorn Tangwiriyakulchai, Varot Techamanoon, Nattawadee Thanasirisopagun, Pimnara Thunyathada, Atiwat Tieanmaungpuk, Ongart Tienngern, Akaphoom Titakasikorn, Pattanee Ukam, Napatson Umpornwattankul, Nicha Utenpitakkul, Jariyawat Vaeteewootacharn, Pakawat Varaphakdi, Paisit Viratigul, Nuntiwa Waiyasith, Kornchawan Waiyasusri, Ibrohem Wangji, Pudit Wichaidit, Chanchai Wimonsirichotikun, Supawai Wongkovit, Ke Xu, Chiahui Yu, Yujun Zou

Project Credits

Ribbon Dance Park
Project title: Ribbon Dance Park
Location: Xi'an, China
Area: 38,000 m²
Completion: 2019
Photography: Holi Landscape Photography, Shiromio Studio, Tothree design

Collaboration
Client: Sunac Group (Xi An)
Architect: gad
Interior: CCD, SCDA
Local team: Shanghai Weimar Landscape
Environment Visual System: Tothree design

TROPSTERS
Design Director: Pok Kobkongsanti
Team: Fusang Ren, Huamei Yin, Yunya Tang, Pitchayut Luadsoongnern

Residence Rabbits
Project title: Residence Rabbits
Location: Bangkok, Thailand
Area: 420 m²
Completion: 2017
Photography: W Workspace

Collaboration
Client: Kobkongsanti Family
Architect: BOONdesign Co., Ltd.
Interior: BOONdesign Co., Ltd., Pok Kobkongsanti

TROPSTERS
Design Director: Pok Kobkongsanti
Team: Pinmanee Lamor, Rahut Lertsopaporn, Theerapong Sanguansripisut

Ashton Chula-Silom
Project title: Ashton Chula-Silom
Location: Bangkok, Thailand
Area: 7,100m²
Completion: 2018
Photography: Ketsiree Wongwan, Ananda Development PLC.

Collaboration
Client: Ananda Development Public Company Limited
Architect: A49
Interior: DWP

TROPSTERS
Design Director: Pok Kobkongsanti
Team: Thongchai Sinsansiri, Supawai Wongkovit, Ongart Tienngern, Kampon Prakobsajakul

An Villa
Project title: An Villa (Vanke Shaoxing)
Location: Shaoxing, China
Area: 6,600 m²
Completion: 2021
Photography: DID Studio, YUAN WEI KANG

Collaboration
Client: Yoland Real Estate Co.Ltd, Newhope, Vanke Group(Hangzhou)
Architect: Allied Architects International
Interior: Matrix Design
Local team: Shanghai Weimar Landscape

TROPSTERS
Design Director: Pok Kobkongsanti
Team: Jayda Zhu. Yuting Lu, Yiping Liu, Huamei Yin, Pengtao Sang, Ke Ma

Veranda Pattaya
Project title: Veranda Pattaya
Location: Chonburi, Thailand
Area: 11,080 m²
Completion: 2016
Photography: Spaceshift Studio

Collaboration
Client: Veranda Resort and Spa Co. Ltd.
Architect: The Office of Bangkok Architects
Interior: August Design

TROPSTERS
Design Director: Pok Kobkongsanti
Team: Paisit Viratigul, Rahut Lertsopaporn

Groove @ Central World
Project title: Groove @ Central World
Location: Bangkok, Thailand
Area: 9,000 m²
Completion: 2013
Photography: Spaceshift Studio

Collaboration
Client: Central Pattana Company Limited
Architect: Synthesis Design + Architecture, A49, FOS

TROPSTERS
Design Director: Pok Kobkongsanti
Team: Maytinee Nakprasert, Pattanee Ukam

Botanica Khao Yai
Project title: Botanica Khao Yai
Location: Nakhon Ratchasima, Thailand
Area: 16,000 m²
Completion: 2015
Photography: Spaceshift Studio

Collaboration
Client: The Scenical Development Company Limited
Architect: Vin Varavarn Architects Co., Ltd.
Interior: Define Studio Co., Ltd.; Mada Design Factory Co., Ltd.

TROPSTERS
Design Director: Pok Kobkongsanti
Team: Peerasit Sangwanloy, Chanchai Wimonsirichotikun

Jing'An Century
Project title: Yanlord Jing'An Century Sales Gallery
Location: Shanghai, China
Area: 2,000 m²
Completion: 2020
Photography: Holi Landscape Photography, Schranimage

Collaboration
Client: Shanghai Yanlord Land
Architect: Tianhua Group
Interior: LWM Architects
Local team: GM Landscape Design

TROPSTERS
Design Director: Pok Kobkongsanti
Team: Fusang Ren, Kehan Zhou, Huamei Yin, Tianheng Xiong

Pyne by Sansiri
Project title: Pyne by Sansiri
Location: Bangkok, Thailand
Area: 2,900 m²
Completion: 2013
Photography: W Workspace, Panoramic Studio

Collaboration
Client: Sansiri Public Company Limited
Architect: Palmer & Turner (Thailand) Co. Ltd.

TROPSTERS
Design Director: Pok Kobkongsanti
Team: Theerapong Sanguansripisut, Ekitsara Meedet, Pattanee Ukam, Naratip Bundi, Tatsaneeya Pasuk, Kampon Prakobsajakul

J Residence
Project title: Jesada Residence
Location: Samutprakarn, Thailand
Area: 6,070 m²
Completion: 2016
Photography: W Workspace

Collaboration
Client: Private owner
Architect: A49HD
Interior: A49HD

TROPSTERS
Design Director: Pok Kobkongsanti
Team: Chonfun Atichat, Pinmanee Lamor, Pattanee Ukam

Ad Lib
Project title: The Garden of Ad Lib Hotel
Location: Bangkok, Thailand
Area: 1,620 m²
Completion: 2014
Photography: W Workspace

Collaboration
Client: Heritage Estates Co., Ltd.
Architect: Tierra Design Bangkok
Interior: August Design

TROPSTERS
Design Director: Pok Kobkongsanti
Team: Kittinai Kittirojana

Quattro by Sansiri
Project title: Quattro by Sansiri
Location: Bangkok, Thailand
Area: 7,200 m²
Completion: 2012
Photography: W Workspace

Collaboration
Client: Sansiri Public Company Limited
Architect: Dhevanand Co., Ltd
Interior: DWP

TROPSTERS
Design Director: Pok Kobkongsanti
Team: Chonfun Atichat, Anuwit Cheewarattanaporn, Nattapong Raktai, Chatchawan Banjongsiri

Urban Green Valley
Project title: Urban Green Valley (Arcadia)
Location: Shanghai, China
Area: 7,700 m²
Completion: 2021
Photography: Holi Landscape Photography

Collaboration
Client: Shanghai Yanlord Land
Architect: GOA + Tianhua Group
Interior: WJID
Local team: Shanghai Weimar Landscape

TROPSTERS
Design Director: Pok Kobkongsanti
Team: Fusang Ren, Kehan Zhou, Huamei Yin, Heidi Liu, Siyi Lu, Pengtao Sang, Ke Ma

Ashton Residence 41
Project title: Ashton 41
Location: Bangkok, Thailand
Area: 3,030 m²
Completion: 2017
Photography: Spaceshift Studio

Collaboration
Client: Ananda Development Public Company Limited
Architect: A49HD
Interior: PIA

TROPSTERS
Design Director: Pok Kobkongsanti
Team: Pin-a-nong La-mor, Supichaya Osothsilp, Chanchai Wimonsirichotikun

Hilton Pattaya
Project title: Hilton Central Pattaya Hotel
Location: Chonburi, Thailand
Area: 4,198 m²
Completion: 2010
Photography: W Workspace, Adam Brozzone, Charkhrit Chartarsa

Collaboration
Client: Central Pattana Public Company Limited
Architect: Department of ARCHITECTURE Co.Ltd.
Interior: Department of ARCHITECTURE Co.Ltd.
Overall concept design: Anon Pairot Design Studio

TROPSTERS
Design Director: Pok Kobkongsanti
Team: Pakawat Varaphakdi, Bun Asai, Wasin Muneepeerakul, Pattarapol Jormkhanngen, Teerayut Pruekpanasan, Chatchawan Banjongsiri

Chiang Rai Residence
Project title: Chiang Rai Residence
Location: Chiang Rai, Thailand
Area: 4,206 m²
Completion: 2020
Photography: W Workspace

Collaboration
Client: Private owner
Architect: A49HD
Interior: A49HD

TROPSTERS
Design Director: Pok Kobkongsanti
Team: Pattaraphol Jomkhangen, Piyakan Kleebthong, Ibrohem Wangji

Ashton Asoke-Rama 9
Project title: Ashton Asoke-Rama 9
Location: Bangkok, Thailand
Area: 2,850 m²
Completion: 2020
Photography: Rungkit Charoenwat

Collaboration
Client: Ananda Development Public Company Limited
Architect: A49
Interior: PIA

TROPSTERS
Design Director: Pok Kobkongsanti
Team: Thongchai Sinsansiri, Paisit Viratigul, Pradit Lertsakul, Kampon Prakobsajjakul

Nana Coffee Roaster Bangna
Project title: Nana Coffee Roaster Bangna
Location: Bangkok, Thailand
Area: 250 m²
Completion: 2022
Photography: W Workspace

Collaboration
Client: Nana Coffee Roaster
Architect: IDIN Architects
Interior: IDIN Architects

TROPSTERS
Design Director: Pok Kobkongsanti
Team: Nicha Utenpitakkul, Piyakan Kleebthong, Thansinee Boonjue

Published in Australia in 2024 by
The Images Publishing Group Pty Ltd
ABN 89 059 734 431

Offices

Melbourne
Waterman Business Centre
Suite 64, Level 2 UL40
1341 Dandenong Rd,
Chadstone, VIC 3148
Australia
Tel: +61 3 8564 8122

New York
6 West 18th Street 4B
New York City, NY 10011
United States
Tel: +1 212 645 1111

Shanghai
6F, Building C, 838 Guangji Road
Hongkou District, Shanghai 200434
China
Tel: +86 021 31260822

books@imagespublishing.com
www.imagespublishing.com

Copyright © The Images Publishing Group Pty Ltd 2024
The Images Publishing Group Reference Number: 1685

All rights reserved. Apart from any fair dealing for the purposes of private study, research, criticism or review as permitted under the Copyright Act, no part of this publication may be reproduced, stored in a retrieval system or transmitted in any form by any means, electronic, mechanical, photocopying, recording or otherwise, without the written permission of the publisher.

All photography is attributed in the Project Credits on pages 254–55 with the following exceptions. Cover: DID Studio (An Villa, Shaoxing, China);
Pages 2–3: ZOE Lighting Design (Yanlord The Times Garden, Hangzhou, China);
Pages 4–5: XF Photography (Yanlord Poetic Villa, Shanghai, China);
Pages 6–7: Holi Landscape Photography (Yanlord on the Park, Shenzhen, China);
Pages 8–9: Holi Landscape Photography (Ribbon Dance Park, Xi'an, China);
Page 12: XF Photography (Yanlord on the Park, Shenzhen, China);
Pages 18–19: W Workspace, Wison Tungthunya (Residence Raintree, Bangkok, Thailand); Page 251: Dsignsomething (Pok Kobkongsanti);
Page 253: Spaceshift Studio (TROP Office, Bangkok, Thailand)

 A catalogue record for this book is available from the National Library of Australia

Title: TROP: terrains + open space
Author: Pok Kobkongsanti with Rebecca Gross (Introduction)
ISBN: 9781864709612

This title was commissioned in IMAGES' Melbourne office and produced as follows:
Editorial Danielle Hampshire; Georgia (Gina) Tsarouhas; Jeanette Wall;
Graphic design Ryan Marshall; *Art direction/production* Nicole Boehringer

Printed on 140gsm Da Dong Woodfree paper (FSC®) in China by Artron Art Group

IMAGES has included on its website a page for special notices in relation to this and its other publications. Please visit www.imagespublishing.com

Every effort has been made to trace the original source of copyright material contained in this book. The publishers would be pleased to hear from copyright holders to rectify any errors or omissions.
The information and illustrations in this publication have been prepared and supplied by TROP. While all reasonable efforts have been made to ensure accuracy, the publishers do not, under any circumstances, accept responsibility for errors, omissions and representations, express or implied.